MAGGIE, EILEEN AND ME

MAGGIE, EILEEN AND ME

MICHAEL NORMAN

Matador
9 Priory Business Park,
Wistow Road, Kibworth Beauchamp,
Leicestershire. LE8 0RX
Tel: 0116 279 2299
Email: books@troubador.co.uk
Web: www.troubador.co.uk/matador
Twitter: @matadorbooks

ISBN 978 1838593 704

British Library Cataloguing in Publication Data.
A catalogue record for this book is available from the British Library.

Printed and bound in Great Britain by 4edge Limited
Typeset in 10pt Minion Pro by Troubador Publishing Ltd, Leicester, UK

Matador is an imprint of Troubador Publishing Ltd

To my dear wife, to whom I am
grateful for suffering me whilst I
suffered others.

Preface

I WAS FORTUNATE TO BE ABLE TO RETIRE IN 2002 IN MY mid-fifties. Later that year, however, my mother began to exhibit early signs of dementia. Within a couple of years, one of her younger sisters did the same. As the relative living nearest to each of them, I had little choice but to assume responsibility for their care. This was particularly onerous for me in the case of my mother as we had had a difficult relationship for many years. As her illness progressed, and unpleasant elements of her personality became more pronounced, that relationship became, at times, toxic.

It had not always been like that. In my childhood and teens, my bond with my mother had been strong, which was fortunate as my father was a seriously dysfunctional parent. But people change, sometimes for the better and sometimes not, as do the dynamics within a family.

A relatively brief family history is contained in Part One of this memoir. Part Two comprises material developments from 2002 to 2016 on an annual basis. It is drawn from my diaries (which I began that year, principally to record my retirement activities, as part of an attempt to ensure that I did not stagnate), and from contemporaneous emails and other correspondence.

Together, these provide a record of the descent of the two sisters into the misery of dementia, and the effect on me of trying to help them.

This memoir is a very personal account, but I hope that it will be of interest to readers outside my immediate family. It may even help them to cope with a variety of problems facing those caring for family members suffering from a cruel and increasingly common illness. Those problems arise not only directly from the illness itself but also indirectly from factors such as the ineptitude of banks and the failings of the National Health Service.

PART ONE

Chapter One

Maggie and Eileen: The Early Years

My maternal grandmother, Elsie, was married twice. In 1918 her first husband, a ship's steward named Fletcher, abandoned her and their three young children, with a fourth on the way. None of them ever saw him again. There were two girls and a boy, the latter being the youngest of the three. The fourth child was another girl. At the time, the family was living in rented furnished accommodation in Portsmouth. Immediately before Fletcher's abrupt departure, he sold most of the landlord's furniture. The family was left destitute. Elsie presumed that her husband was going back to sea and so, with her children in tow, she went to the docks where the ship on which he had last served was berthed. He was not on board but, on learning of her plight, the crew had a whip-round to provide some temporary financial aid.

Elsie was in a desperate state. Capable only of menial work, she was clearly unable to support all of her children and was faced with the heart-rending decision of putting them in care. A wealthy aunt was prepared to take the eldest daughter, but Elsie did not want to separate the two girls, and so they were put into a Church of England orphanage. The boy stayed with his mother, as did the youngest daughter after she was born. At the age of 14 months she went to live with one of Elsie's cousins who had been unable to have a child of her own. The two elder girls, Edith and Mary, were unhappy over the way they had been treated and, perhaps unsurprisingly, remained somewhat embittered, even in adulthood, particularly Edith.

After a couple of years or so, Elsie met my maternal grandfather, George Rowe, a non-commissioned officer in the army. He was in his early forties and was separated from his wife, with whom he had had three children. George and Elsie met in a pub where she was employed to do the washing-up. She and her son were living in accommodation above. George later recounted that she was so poor that her one pair of shoes was falling apart.

My mother, Maggie, would sometimes tell me about the circumstances of her mother's early life. Probably the last time she did so was after I had entered the legal profession. She was vague about the time that had passed between Fletcher's disappearance and her parents' meeting and subsequent marriage. She said that Fletcher had gone missing and had been declared dead. I pointed out to her that, in the absence of any other evidence, there could be no presumption of death until a person had been missing for seven years. I suggested that she could have been born before the seven years had elapsed and made a joke that she might have been a "little bastard." She did not find this even slightly amusing and I suspected that I had hit a raw spot. Illegitimacy bore a considerable social stigma at the time she was born. It is only recently that I have discovered that my suspicion was well-founded. Her parents were unable to marry until 18 months after my mother's birth. Not only had the seven years not expired but also George and his wife had not divorced. In the event, a divorce was unnecessary as the wife died in 1925, or thereabouts.

Unlike Fletcher, George was a good man. He continued to see the two sons of his first marriage periodically (a daughter having died in childhood) and provided them with some financial support. After his first wife died, George's younger son went to live with him and Elsie. George even sent money from time to time to Edith and Mary.

My mother was born in 1924. Some eighteen months later, the second daughter, Eileen, arrived. Their parents had married six weeks earlier.

In the late 1920s, my grandfather's regiment was posted to Egypt and the family moved with him.

Whilst in Egypt, Eileen damaged her kidneys. She was bouncing on a bed and fell off. As a consequence, she was ill for several months. Her father was with her at the time of the accident and it seems that he blamed himself for it. Thereafter he tended to spoil Eileen, who apparently became a bit of a brat. For example, whenever my mother had a birthday, Eileen had to have a present too.

The two girls were educated in Alexandria at a French convent school and, as a matter of necessity, they became fluent in French. If you need to leave the room to go to the lavatory, it helps to know how to ask. The school was run by nuns and discipline was strictly enforced. My mother knuckled down and performed well academically; Aunt Eileen did neither and would occasionally escape to the family home during school hours, from which she would be dragged back by her mother struggling and weeping. She was clearly somewhat scarred by her experiences at school as she would often recount them to me, even when she was an old lady. She said that the nuns were physically cruel, although she was fond of one of the younger ones and, for a while, thought of taking the veil herself.

During the family's time in Egypt, the third and fourth daughters were born. They were named June and Angela. My mother was 13 years old when Angela was born. Both of them say that Maggie was a kind and helpful big sister. It was said that June used to follow her around like a pet dog.

About the time of my mother's 15th birthday, in early 1939, she became unofficially engaged to an army officer who was almost twice her age. Shortly thereafter, the Rowe family transferred back to England and took up residence in a flat in London. This led to the demise of the romance and my mother was distraught when she heard that her beau had found someone new. I only learned of this piece of family history quite recently from my aunt, Angela.

With the benefit of hindsight, the family's return to England was not a wise move. Later that year, Hitler's army invaded Poland and, on 3rd September, Britain declared war on Germany. A year later the Blitz began with London being bombed almost every day and night for 11 weeks. My mother told me how she hated the nightly visits to an air raid shelter and, after a while, adopting a fatalistic approach, refused to leave her bed. Fortunately, the building never suffered a direct hit.

During the course of the war the family relocated to Middlesex and Maggie found employment as a librarian. Eileen worked in an armaments factory, assembling shells.

It was while working at a library in Middlesex that my mother first met my father, Maurice, who was a regular visitor there. He was unmarried, bespectacled, balding, and an asthmatic (for which reason he had been rejected for military service). She was petite (no more than five feet tall in her bare feet) and pretty. He was 41 and she was 19. Superficially, at least, it seems a strange match. He had, however, an outgoing personality, was a man of the world, had his own business and was widely travelled. She, on the other hand, had had a sheltered upbringing, was quite shy, and was probably flattered by the attentions of a comparatively sophisticated man. It may also have been significant that her father, of whom she was very fond, was in his early forties when Maggie was born, and it seems from her romance in Egypt that she liked older men. Anyway, after a relatively short courtship, they married in the last year of the war, when she was 21 years old. This was despite her father indicating concern over the match. It was my mother who told me about that, although she dismissed it, claiming he was always unhappy at the prospect of one of his daughters leaving home. I suspect that this was a case of her believing what she wanted to believe and that the concern was more to do with the age gap, Maurice's personality, or both.

At the time of her marriage, my mother had very long chestnut hair, which was pinned up at the back in a bun. It was so long that she was able to sit on it. She used to recount an incident that occurred when she took me to a funfair when I was about eight years old. We were on a ride called The Whip which whizzed round so fast that her hairpins came out, causing her bun to fall apart. As far as I can remember, she retained her long hair until her early thirties, when she adopted a shorter hairstyle which I thought looked much better. Her hair went grey at quite an early age, possibly in her late thirties, but she did not colour it. Even when it was completely white, she still looked young for her age.

I think my mother was almost certainly a virgin when she married. Her parents were very protective, and my father used to recall how, when he took her to the cinema during their courtship, her mother came along as a chaperone. That must have been fun. Hopefully she didn't sit between them.

A conversation I have had recently with Angela has been enlightening. She and June were schoolgirls when my mother got married and they used to visit her at weekends. She looked forward to their visits and they gained the impression that she was lonely. The view in the Rowe family was that Maurice was a controlling man and a hard taskmaster; indeed, Eileen used to refer to him as a Svengali. They thought that Maggie was frightened of him and sometimes seemed depressed. Angela recalls Maggie telling her that she had to dry nappies inside the house as Maurice would not allow her to dry them on the outside washing line. She also remembers Maggie giving her and June a tea towel to take home to their mother (because of the war, these were in short supply), but imploring them not to let Maurice know. These days my father would probably have been regarded as a control freak.

I have also learned that Maurice was occasionally rude to George. Elsie asked her husband why he put up with it, and he said that he did it for Maggie's sake.

I was born 18 months after my parents' marriage, and my brother, Tom, three years after that.

CHAPTER TWO
MAGGIE AND MAURICE AS PARENTS

WHEN TOM AND I WERE CHILDREN, MUM WAS A VERY good mother. She loved us, looked after us well and was interested in what we did. Dad, on the other hand, was singularly unsuited to be the father of sons. He had not enjoyed a good relationship with his own father and, as a young man, had cleared off to Australia. This was following the example of his older brother, Harry, who had gone to South America. Their father had apparently been a narrow-minded disciplinarian. Sadly, my father did not learn from his own experiences. Although he was far from strait-laced, he was set in his ways and would rarely tolerate any opinion within the family that did not accord with his own.

As a father he was the opposite of a role model. His parenting skills were almost non-existent. Whilst parent-child relations have undoubtedly changed during my lifetime, with parents enjoying a closer relationship with their offspring than was the case when my generation were children, my father was a particularly strict and remote parent. He was an anachronism in that he behaved in many ways like a Victorian father, even though he was born a year after the queen's death and was 44 years old when I was born. As a consequence, I don't think he derived much pleasure from his children.

Dad wanted a daughter and was disappointed when his second child was another son. If he had had a daughter I suspect she would have been spoiled rotten. He was fond of Angela, my mother's youngest sister, who was only 10 when I was born. She remembers him taking her shopping in London for clothes around that time. He also offered to pay for her to have dancing lessons.

My earliest memory of my father is of sitting on his knee, when I was probably no more than two years old, while he read me nursery rhymes. That is the only time I remember him reading to either me or Tom. Indeed, he joined in few of our boyhood activities. I do recall him helping me ride a bike when I was five or six. Another occasion was when he bought us a large second-hand train set for Christmas a few years later. Later still, he joined in a game of tennis for about 15 minutes and spent about the same amount of time at cricket. We did, however, sometimes play Kalooki (a form of rummy) as a family and he attempted, on one occasion, to teach us, and Mum, the rudiments of bridge. Unfortunately, he became stroppy when we appeared not to be taking it sufficiently seriously.

I think that, because of his age, he had the attitude, probably inherited from his father, that children should be seen and not heard, and that anything connected with childcare fell entirely within the domain of the mother. Fortunately, Maggie was a caring and patient mother. Through her efforts I was able to read before I started school. Later, if asked, she would help with homework. He never did.

My cousin Maurice, named after my father by his brother, Harry, recently told Tom and me that he could not recall his father ever hugging him. This made me realise that I could not remember my father ever hugging me either.

Our father rarely showed any great interest in what Tom and I were doing. When we returned from school in the early evening, he would merely enquire whether we had had a good day. We would reply in the affirmative, even if that had not been the case, and that was the end of the conversation. Even when I was away at university and would occasionally ring home, he would go and fetch my mother so that she could talk to me. He had nothing to ask and nothing to say to me of any consequence. When Tom and I were growing up, he did not discuss things with us. Instead he would talk down to us or lecture us. He would often be sarcastic and gave the impression that our views were of little consequence. One of his occasional comments to me was that I "talked for the sake of talking." I don't think that I was a particularly loquacious child; it was more a case of him not being interested in what I had to say.

Dad was an irritable man whose moods could fluctuate quite rapidly. I often seemed to be a cause of his irritation and he would lose his temper with me over trivial things. I would sometimes seek comfort, or an explanation, from my mother and she told me, on more than one occasion, that he was jealous of me. In fact, Angela has told me that this was a view held by the Rowe family. My grandmother apparently expressed the opinion that Maurice should never have had children as he was temperamentally unsuited to be a father. This jealousy thing did not make a lot of sense to me when I was young but, as I grew older, I could see that he probably regarded me as a rival for my mother's attention or, possibly, affection. He did not show similar animosity towards Tom. Presumably Tom did not annoy him as much as I did. I do not believe that I went out of my way to annoy him. I often felt that he had criticised me unjustly and would say so. He would not tolerate being contradicted. As far as he was concerned, I was a 'cheeky little bastard.' Tom was more careful not to do or say anything that might annoy his father. He was also protected by being the younger child in that it is usually the older one who has to fight the battles on behalf of himself and his siblings. It was obvious to members of my mother's family that he was his father's favourite. The first occasion of favouritism I can remember was when I was 11 and Tom was eight My father had an oil painting made of Tom. He subsequently arranged for the same artist to make a pencil drawing of me. It could not have been made clearer that one child was being preferred over the other.

It is difficult for anyone to look back to their childhood and view their behaviour objectively. I accept that I was cheeky on occasions, but I do not believe that I was excessively rude to either parent. Indeed, my father had such a bad temper that, as a child, I tended to be wary of him. I am, moreover, reassured by Angela telling me recently that "Maurice was very hard on you." He would also take little or no account of my age. I can recall watching horse racing on the TV with my mother one afternoon. I was probably about six at the time. It was not that either of us was particularly keen on the sport of kings; it was more a case, in those early days of black and white television, that there was not much else to watch in the afternoon. I correctly predicted the winner of a race (as likely as not on the scientific basis of liking the horse's name), and proudly told my daddy of this when he returned home later that day. He reacted angrily, which upset me because I could not understand what I had done wrong. My mother explained later that it was because he was worried that I would turn out to be a gambler. I was six years old; I probably didn't even know what gambling meant. I mentioned this incident recently to Tom and it made sense to him as he recalled that Dad had an account with a well-known bookmaker who he would occasionally telephone to place a bet. Whilst I am confident that he was not a problem gambler, the incident demonstrates that he had not got a clue of how to bring up children.

I can remember another example of my father's failure to take my age into account. I had enjoyed playing cricket from childhood and, at about the age of nine, I expressed the ambition of one day playing for England. Several years later, after it had become only too apparent that my childish wish would never come close to being realised, he sneeringly threw it back in my face.

Another incident that is etched in my memory occurred when I was about 11. My father hit me several times on the hand with a cane as a punishment for some offence I had committed. This took place in the kitchen, by the back door, and was in the presence of my mother, Tom and 'the maid' (one of a series of women, usually young, who were employed to help my mother in the house). He clearly did this in front of an audience to humiliate me as, after being hit, I went off into the garden, and he called after me something along the lines of "Now you can go and cry."

My father earned a living principally from seasonal catering. He rented a café near where we first lived in Surrey. When the tenancy expired, and the renewal terms were felt to be too onerous, he took a tenancy of another café, this time in Kent. He moved into digs there while the rest of us continued to live in the family home until it was sold. At that stage we went into a rented flat in Kent while my parents looked for a new property. The one they eventually bought was a large five-bedroomed house with an acre of garden. I lived there from the age of seven and throughout my teenage years.

My father was very much the master of the house and, in my early childhood, I do not recall Mum ever taking issue with him. She worked hard as a mother and housewife. When we moved to the house in Kent, my parents employed a cleaning lady two or three mornings a week, but Mum still did her fair share of the cleaning as well as all the cooking and the ironing.

A few years later my father took a tenancy of a second café in Kent, about 12 miles from where we lived. The trade there was also seasonal; the cafés were only open from late spring to early autumn. My parents ran that business for about ten years, after which my father acquired a newsagent/confectioner/tobacconist shop a few miles from our home. I have occasionally wondered how my father could have afforded to live in such a large house, educate his children privately and enjoy a very comfortable standard of living. On the one hand, the cafés were situated in leisure parks by a river and could get very busy during the summer months, particularly in school holidays. On the other hand, trade could be significantly affected by the inclement weather for which English summers are notorious. The businesses generated a lot of cash and I suspect that not all the income was declared for tax purposes. Moreover, my father was not a saver; most of his capital was tied up in the house.

Ironically, for someone engaged in catering, my father could not cook. In fact, he did very little at home to help his wife. The only jobs I can recall him doing were emptying and refilling the coke-fuelled Aga (before it was changed to an oil model), drying up after a meal, occasionally dead-heading the roses, or watering areas of the garden in a dry spell. He was possibly the laziest person I have ever come across. He did not even write his own business letters, his excuse being that his handwriting was illegible. Perhaps he thought that using a typewriter was beneath him. This was another task that was left to my mother.

During the period from mid-October to early April, when the cafés were closed, Dad assumed no additional domestic duties. He didn't even occupy himself in the garden. That was left to one or two part-time gardeners. Owing to his highly-strung nature, he seemed unable to sit down for long and always appeared to be in a hurry. If the phone rang, he would run to answer it; if he needed to go upstairs, he would run rather than walk. My mother used to say that he was busy doing nothing. If he did some minor task for which he earned Maggie's thanks, he would often say "A little help is worth a ton of pity"; this was said without any irony.

The larger of the two cafés in Kent was run by a very capable manageress, Mrs Smith. My father used to put in an appearance for a short while in the morning and would return in the early evening to cash up. He was involved to some extent in ordering food for the business, although Mrs Smith would have been perfectly capable of doing that. I sometimes got the impression that she regarded his presence as unnecessary. When she eventually left my father's employment, she became the catering manager for a substantial manufacturing company.

The smaller café was also run by a manageress, although she was not of the same calibre as Mrs Smith. This meant that my father had to be more hands-on. I believe that he dealt with ordering the food, but he visited the premises comparatively rarely. That job was delegated to my mother. She had to go there several times a week, and possibly daily during the summer school holidays. In the early days, before we owned a car, the journey there involved her catching a bus to the station, then a train journey and another bus ride at the other end. This would probably have taken about an hour door to door. The return journey would have been quicker as she would get a taxi from the station to home. This was because she was carrying the day's takings in a shopping bag. It was extraordinarily risky for such a small woman to be travelling alone carrying large amounts of cash. I do not remember her complaining about her lot; she just got on with it.

It was principally because of my mother's involvement in the business that my father employed what was rather grandly referred to as a 'maid' to help in the house. This was in addition to the cleaning lady. The maid used to prepare breakfast for Tom and me and then cook our evening meal when our mother was at work.

Although Maggie was a good mother during my childhood, on thinking about it now there was an aspect of it which I find puzzling. Tom and I quite often went to stay with an elderly lady named Mrs Inman for a week or more during school holidays. She had been my father's housekeeper when he lived in Surrey before he married. Mum would take us to Mrs Inman's by train and then collect us at the end of the stay. Mrs Inman was no longer working; her husband was a gardener. They owned their own semi-detached house where they lived with their adult, adopted daughter, who suffered from schizophrenia. Tom and I loved Mrs Inman, and she loved us. We were much closer to her than to our grandmother and enjoyed going to stay with her. She took us by coach to the seaside, or by bus to the cinema, or on other excursions. Otherwise we kept ourselves amused, or we would play cards or board games with the family. On one occasion she took us to Butlin's at Clacton for a week and, on another, to that exotic resort, Canvey Island. What I find puzzling, is why we stayed with her so often. I recall one stay of about three weeks when our parents went on a cruise. I was 11 at the time and Tom was eight. There is no way that my wife, Anna, and I would have gone away on holiday without our children. I feel almost certain that it would have been my father's idea, but

I am surprised that my mother agreed to it. This was probably a case of her being compliant with her husband's wishes. It is possible that one or more of the other visits may have been arranged so that our parents could take a short holiday. Alternatively, they (or more likely, just my father) may have felt like taking an extended break from us. Again, there is no way that Anna and I would have wanted to do that. There were only two occasions when our children were little that we went away for a weekend without them. They stayed with my parents both times. In fact, it was only our daughter, Sarah, the first time as our son, Andrew, had not been born then. This did not prevent my mother, who as she grew older developed a tendency to hyperbole, from telling people how she used to look after our children when they were young.

I remember, as a young child, being taken to Brittany by my parents. What I had forgotten was that Tom, who was a baby at the time, had been left at home, being cared for by Elsie. He was at the stage where he was able to sit but was not yet crawling. I have learned that Elsie was happy to look after him, as she loved babies, but nevertheless was quite shocked that my mother had chosen to go away without him. Again, I suppose that she was being compliant with her husband's wishes.

Life became easier for Mum when Dad bought a car. This was after she passed her driving test, following several failed attempts, at about the age of 41. I passed mine around the same time. Before then we had used public transport or taxis. Dad had an account with a local taxi firm for years. He showed no inclination to drive. He maintained that he had done a lot of driving during his time in Australia and had no wish to do so in England where he considered the roads to be too crowded. He had returned home before the war. Compared with Australia, the roads would have been busy, but hardly crowded. I have read that there were 2.5 million cars on British roads in 1934. By December 2018 there were 38.2 million vehicles licensed for use on the roads of Great Britain. Either he was nervous of driving or, more likely, he couldn't be bothered. Having bought a car, he had his wife to act as his chauffeuse.

The fact that my father did not drive did not prevent him being a particularly irritating backseat driver. One of his annoying habits was to remind the driver about the choke. In those days cars had manual chokes. The choke had to be pulled out to enable the car to start in cold weather, and then gradually pushed in as the air/fuel ratio was reached. The whole procedure would only take a few minutes. If the choke was pushed back too soon, the engine could stall. If it was left out too long, the engine would 'flood' and it could take a long time to re-start. If my father was a passenger when I was driving, he would almost invariably mention the choke, usually to enquire whether I had pushed it back in. On one occasion, towards the end of a journey of two hours or so, I could not resist asking him whether I could now push the choke in. Mum and Tom were also in the car. They found it funny. Dad did not.

There was another occasion when I went to collect him from the café early one evening. He asked me to take Mrs Smith home first and then proceeded to give me the most obvious directions, even though I knew perfectly well where she lived, having been to her flat on earlier occasions. When I saw her subsequently, she made a joke about it, giving me instructions on how to find my way home.

After living in our big house for a few years, my father arranged for a local barber to call there once a fortnight. This was presumably to avoid the bother of having his hair cut in the town. For a man so follically challenged, he was very particular about the hair that remained. The problem was that, to make it worth the barber's while to make the journey, Tom and I had to have our hair cut as well. This became a regular source of friction within the family as we neither needed nor wanted our hair cutting that often. The barber, moreover, was not exactly a stylist. His speciality was a 'short back and sides.' It was not until I reached the sixth form at school that this routine came to an end and I could grow my hair longer.

My father also tended to snobbishness. His embargo on hanging nappies on the washing line is, probably, an example of this. When we were living in rented accommodation after first moving to Kent, I made friends with several boys who lived in the locality and we used to play together outside. My father indicated that some of them were not the sort of boys I should be mixing with. I think that the basis for his objection was their diction being less than perfect. Subsequently, whilst Tom and I were at primary school, he insisted on us having private elocution lessons. Neither of us was badly-spoken and I never understood why he considered those lessons to be necessary. Later he sent us to a minor public school that was several miles from our home and involved a door to door journey of about 50 minutes. We could have gone to the local grammar school which was less than a ten-minute walk away. It was also a better school academically. I doubt that he ever gave much thought to sending us to the grammar school. It was only after I left school that I got to know a group of former pupils from there and they were very good company.

My aunt Angela has told me of another incident that sounds as if it may have been attributable to snobbery and is also probably an instance of my mother having been influenced by my father. This occurred in 1960, when Angela was in a very advanced state of pregnancy. She and my uncle Roy called at my parents' house one afternoon to collect some baby's clothes that they had left there. My mother answered the door, told them that the bank manager was visiting and kept them waiting on the doorstep while she went off to collect the clothes. Angela was very hurt by that. The least my mother could have done was to invite them inside while she fetched the clothes. If the bank manager was there on business, which I think was unlikely, then it would not have been essential for Mum to have been present. She could have spent some time with her sister. If the bank manager was on a social visit, which is more likely as he and my father were friends, then why exclude Angela and Roy? They were not exactly social undesirables. Something else Angela told me indicates that my father could not be bothered to make an effort with them. She said that if he was on his own in a room with them, he was unable or unwilling to hold a conversation. He would jump up and say he would go and get Maggie.

Although Dad was a difficult man to live with, he adored his wife and, to use Eileen's words, he 'put her on a pedestal.' He lavished gifts on her, including expensive jewellery and fur coats. He was not, however, particularly generous with Tom and me and, in some ways, was quite mean. He was particularly tight-fisted over use of the telephone. We could not use the phone without first asking permission and, even then, he would make a fuss if we used it for more than a few minutes.

My father's regard for my mother is illustrated by an incident that I have learned of only recently. Edith, my mother's eldest half-sister, who was regarded within the family as a troublemaker, brought up the subject of Maggie's illegitimacy in front of Dad. My mother was mortified as he had not been informed of this. His reaction was to put a protective arm around his wife and make it clear that it was not something that bothered him.

When I was young, I also adored Mum and was proud of her. She was pretty and younger than any of my friends' mothers. When my parents came to my school's annual prize-giving day, she seemed to me to be the most glamorous mother there. She always looked smart; being tiny, most of her clothes were created for her by a dressmaker. I remember thinking, as a child, how good it was to have such a young mother. It came as a shock to both me and Tom when we first discovered that she was not a perfect person. This happened on a family holiday one summer when I was about 13. We were out for the evening and Mum was wearing a new dress. Dad asked us what we thought of it. That was not a sensible question to ask of young boys who had not learned to be tactful and who were ignorant of women's fashions. We both indicated that we did not much like the dress. Instead of laughing it off, Mum became cross and rather spiteful. Dad weighed in too, telling her to take no notice of us as we were just stupid little boys (or something similar). Mum's reaction was such that both Tom and I can still remember the incident sixty years later.

By my teens I had begun to stand up to my father to a greater extent. My relationship with him deteriorated after he bought the newsagent business. I would have been about 15 then. The shop was run by a manageress who lived in a flat above it with her husband. Dad used to go there on a Sunday morning to check on the week's takings. Afterwards he would call in at the Conservative Club and would have a beer or two. He was not much of a drinker and had a strange affectation that 'gentlemen don't drink pints,' only halves.

He would then have an aperitif before lunch and wine with the meal. Over lunch he became truculent and would try to pick an argument, often (but not exclusively) regarding music. He loathed the contemporary pop and rock that Tom and I listened to and would refer to it as 'crap', comparing it unfavourably with the music of the 1920s which, he opined, would still be played in 40 years' time, unlike, say, the songs of the Beatles, who he regarded as talentless. (My father was, indubitably, a paragon of tolerance, a lover of contemporary culture, and a veritable prophet.) He would be deliberatively provocative and, when he failed to get a response from me, he would keep on until I reacted. An argument would then ensue, and he would lose his temper. His behaviour was as infantile as it was predictable. Tom has told me that he and Mum used to dread Sunday lunchtimes. By that time, she had got better at standing up to her husband and would not automatically take his side. This made him worse, and he would quite often leave the room and sulk for several days, not speaking to Tom and me, save to say to me, "I hope you're happy now, you little bastard, that your mother and I have had a row."

I well remember a fearful row we had one lunchtime after the editor of the local newspaper had come around for drinks with his wife. I would have been about 17 at the time. This journalist was full of himself. I think my father knew him from the Conservative Club. His name was not one with which I was familiar and so I don't think he was someone my father knew well. Anyway, I mentioned over a delayed lunch something to the effect that the man appeared very conceited and enjoyed talking about himself. This caused my father to go off on a rant saying "Who the bloody hell do you think you are? How dare you criticise a friend of mine." He worked himself into a rage, which was not helped when Mum indicated that she agreed with me. I think that this was one of the occasions when Dad stormed out of the dining room and went into self-imposed exile for several days.

At some stage it appears that my father was advised to try to control his temper by counting to ten if he felt himself getting angry. Instead of doing this internally, he would start to count aloud. He would sit there, at the meal table (our usual battleground), and start: "One, two, three…" I understood the object of the exercise but could not always understand the reason for his anger. Besides which, the exercise was itself provocative. I remember, on one of these occasions, when I didn't think I had said anything to upset him, asking with faux innocence, "Why are you counting?" He lost his temper well before reaching ten.

On more than one occasion, after my father had been particularly unpleasant, Mum would tell Tom and me that he was really very proud of us. I remember responding "Why doesn't he show it then?"

When it came to apply to universities, I restricted my choices to ones that were sufficiently far away that there could be no expectation on me to come home for the weekend. This was possibly a bit rough on Mum, but I seriously don't think Dad was at all bothered about not seeing me for weeks at a time.

Whilst writing this, I am very conscious of producing what could be regarded as an unbalanced portrait of my father. The sad thing is that I am struggling to recall sharing joyous moments with him. One such occasion was while watching the 1966 World Cup final on the television during the university summer vacation. He and I watched it together; Tom was not present for a reason I cannot recall, and I think Mum only watched sporadically. Dad used to smoke quite heavily, and I had started the habit whilst away from home, albeit not heavily. We got through a fair few fags during the match, he did not lecture me about it (which would have been hypocritical) and I enjoyed his company. It is possible that things improved for a while about that time, but it was only a lull in hostilities.

It was during my articles to a firm of solicitors that my relationship with my father reached its nadir. I was living at home at the time and commuting daily to London. It was in this period that I started going out with a local girl named Cathy. She was pretty and bright, having been educated at the girls' grammar school. She too was working in London, as a secretary/PA. It transpired that her father was a delivery driver. When my parents discovered this, they made their disapproval of the relationship abundantly clear. It was immaterial to them that she was a sweet girl. Matters were not assisted by a cringe-worthy mistake I made. Cathy and I had been intimate late one evening on the sofa in the dining room after my parents had gone to bed. I wrapped the used condom in a paper handkerchief and put it under the sofa, intending to retrieve and dispose of it later. Unfortunately, I forgot, only for my mother to discover it several days later when cleaning the room. Both parents were annoyed about it and I was apologetic and embarrassed. I should explain that my father was broad-minded over matters of a sexual nature (provided it was heterosexual) and would not have been surprised to learn that Cathy and I were having sex. His reaction was, however, very strange; he accused me of leaving the condom under the sofa deliberately so that my mother would discover it. I told him that that was a ridiculous suggestion and he lost his temper. This may have been the occasion when he and I had a fight. If it was not then, it would have been about that time. Tom was away at college and did not witness it. Anyway, my father became so angry that he went to hit me. I grabbed his arm, wrestled him to the floor and sat on his chest until he had calmed down. While this was going on my mother was screaming at us to stop.

I cannot now remember whether it was before or after that incident that my parents gave me an ultimatum: if I married Cathy I would be disinherited. This reinforced my belief that my father was a snob. Unfortunately, my mother appeared to be in full agreement with him over my relationship with Cathy and I found this particularly upsetting. I also believe it showed them to be lacking in judgment. In my mother's case, this was probably due to her sheltered upbringing. Cathy was by no means my first girlfriend; she and I had not been going out very long and had never even discussed marriage. Wise parents would have said nothing and let matters take their course. Because of their attitude, I left home and moved to a flat in south London with Cathy and three others. For several months I had no contact with either of my parents. That didn't bother me as far as my father was concerned, but I was unhappy at being alienated from my mother. Eventually Cathy and I broke up and I moved into a bedsit in central London, which I struggled to afford. After a while I was reconciled with my parents and moved back home.

When Tom started his articles in London, Dad decided to help us buy a flat. He had seen in a newspaper that a flat in northwest London was for sale at what seemed to be the remarkably low price of £3,500. This figure seems ridiculous in today's prices but that was not the case then. He said he would lend us £2,000 (approximately £26,000 in today's money) and we could raise the balance by mortgaging the property. At his prompting, Tom and I went to look at the flat during an extended weekday lunchtime. We were wholly inexperienced when it came to buying property, yet Dad left the process entirely to us. He did not see fit to view it himself or suggest we should have a survey carried out. Looking at it in retrospect, I can only attribute this extraordinarily cavalier attitude to his inherent laziness. Anyway, it turned out that there were good reasons for the property to be priced at such a low level: it was in a depressed area and it backed onto a railway line. This latter fact totally escaped our notice, although that was not quite as strange as it sounds. The rear garden was very overgrown, and the railway could not clearly be seen from the flat. We made a major mistake in not asking to view the garden. Possibly even worse was that we had travelled to the local station, had walked from there to the property, yet did not think to investigate its proximity to the railway. It did not take long to realise the mistake we had made. On our first night there I was awoken in the early hours by what sounded like a major car crash. There was not much to see from my bedroom window, apart from some bright lights. With an insouciance which I am now embarrassed to recall, I went back to sleep, only to be awakened a short while later by another loud noise. By this time even I realised that it was unlikely that there would be two car crashes in the vicinity of the property in such a short space of time. It transpired that the property backed on to a shunting yard. Thereafter I went to bed wearing earplugs.

Looking back at these events almost 50 years later, I do wonder what motivated my father to lend us the money. Whilst it was undoubtedly much appreciated by Tom and myself at the time, and I am sure he wanted to help us to get on the property ladder, I cannot help thinking that he probably also saw the opportunity of getting us (particularly me) out of the family home.

Tom and I sold the flat after about a year, moved home for a while and then bought a flat in Finchley, a more salubrious part of northwest London. As it turned out, I only lived there for about a year. During the space of four and a half months, I met and married Anna and moved into her flat in Central London. I sold my interest in the Finchley property to Tom.

Anna was also a solicitor and so my parents had no basis for objecting to her on class grounds. They did not, however, go out of their way to make her feel welcome. This was particularly the case with my mother. Several incidents come to mind.

As a wedding present, my father released me from the obligation to repay him my half of the money he had lent for the purchase of the original flat. This was generous, and I was grateful. It was, however, personal to me and not even a small gift was made to Anna. Her parents were both dead and the wedding was paid for by her older sister and brother. For this reason, we restricted the invitations to close relatives and a few of Anna's family's friends. As far as I am aware, my parents did not even offer to contribute to the cost of the wedding.

Anna and I married in early December 1973. We spent Christmas that year with my parents at the family home. We drove down from London with Tom, probably during the afternoon of Christmas Eve. We discovered that Dad was in bed, unwell. Within a short space of time of our arrival my mother got the hump over something and would barely speak to any of us. None of us had any idea as to which of us or what had upset her, and she refused to talk about it. That evening she declined to eat with us and had her meal with my father in their bedroom. My poor wife, who had been married for less than a month, was experiencing mother-in-law problems at a very early stage. Fortunately, as far as I can recall, the rest of that Christmas passed without further unpleasantness. More, however, was to follow.

The furniture at the Finchley property had come from a self-contained flat forming part of my parents' house. They had let it for many years to a succession of tenants but, by the time I got married, it was no longer occupied. When we married, Anna and I were at an early stage of our respective careers and were not financially well off. I agreed with Tom that I could take the double bed, in which I had slept, to Anna's flat but he would retain the rest of the furniture. My parents were angry when they found out about this, believing that we had been unfair to Tom, and made their feelings clear to both Anna and me. We did not think they were justified in doing so and I felt particularly irked that they had included Anna in their hostility.

In retrospect, I believe that the beginning of the deterioration of my relationship with my mother began about the time of my marriage or, possibly, earlier when I was with Cathy. The dynamics within a family change as the children grow up. There is a major transition when the children become adults themselves and attain financial independence and, again, when they marry. Whereas my father adapted well to these later changes, I don't believe that my mother did. I think she was resentful that her status within the family had altered. She had less influence and, moreover, was no longer the only woman.

Tom and I would call our parents 'Mum' and 'Dad'. Anna, being a polite person, asked my mother what she would like to be called. The response was "I would like you to call me 'Mother'," which I thought was overly formal, but I made no comment. God forbid that she would have suggested that Anna call her by her first name. From then on, I tended to call her 'Mother' as well. Later, after our children, Sarah and Andrew, were born, Anna enquired as to how she would like them to address her. She said she would like to be called 'Grandmother'. I do not know any grandparent who sought that degree of formality. Anyway, it was too long a word for young children and they simply called her 'Gran'. That form of address persisted for the rest of her life.

In his seventies, my father began to suffer badly from arteriosclerosis, as a result of which he had both legs amputated within about 18 months of each other, one just above the knee, the other just below. He was unable to manage with prostheses and was confined to a wheelchair for the remaining eight or nine years of his life. He bore his handicap bravely but was, of course, even more dependent on my mother. One of the less than pleasant tasks she had to perform was to dress the wounds on his stumps every day for a considerable period.

My father noticeably mellowed during his seventies, particularly after he lost his legs. This was presumably part of the ageing process. His attitude towards me improved considerably after I had qualified as a solicitor. He treated me with respect and was interested in my career. Of course, by that time Tom and I were adults, and our father was a man who was clearly able to relate better to adults. I remember one occasion, when my parents were living in East Sussex, and probably over Christmas, when Tom and I took our father to the local pub before dinner. He was then in a wheelchair. He was good company and enjoyed hearing about what we were doing in life. It is so sad that it took him until the last few years of his life to become a normal father.

After Dad lost his legs it became necessary for my parents to move to a new house. He could not climb the stairs and there was no bathroom downstairs. I also think they had to move for financial reasons as most of their capital was tied up in the house. They had already given up both catering businesses, leaving only the newsagent/confectioner/ tobacconist shop. With my father being handicapped, that had to be sold. It was largely left to Mother to do the house hunting and they ended up relocating to East Sussex. It seemed to me a bizarre decision as it involved leaving the area in which they had lived for over 20 years and in which they had made several friends. It also moved them further away from their sons. Tom was still in London; Anna and I had moved to Surrey and had started a family.

The East Sussex property was part of an oast house that had been converted into three houses. It was undoubtedly attractive, and property was considerably less expensive than where they had moved from, so they were able to realise some capital. Having said that, the property was not suitable for a man in a wheelchair. To accommodate my father, it was necessary to install a lift from the entrance hall to a bedroom on the first floor. This involved losing space in the bedroom and did nothing to enhance its appearance. Moreover, the house had a step between the dining hall and the lounge which necessitated my mother manoeuvring the wheelchair up and down. There was also a set of three steps on the landing, separating two of the bedrooms from the other two. I don't think that Dad ever got to see the two further rooms.

As my father became a markedly more pleasant person in his old age, my much-younger mother went in the opposite direction. She became excessively talkative and her hypersensitivity (an early example of which was her reaction to her young sons' failure to admire her dress) became more apparent. Perhaps she had always talked a lot; if so, I had not been aware of it. I think my father used to dominate the conversation and this kept her loquaciousness under control. It seemed that as he became calmer and spoke less, she seized the opportunity to fill the airwaves. The fact that she had little of interest to say did not stop her saying it, and at length. To make matters worse, she developed an annoying habit of purporting to repeat a conversation verbatim, even though the original conversation might have taken place years earlier. It reminded Tom and me of a comedy sketch, possibly from *Monty Python*, of two old ladies having an intensely tedious conversation (" 'Well…' I said. 'Yes' she said.") It became apparent on one occasion that my father was aware of how wearisome her conversation could be. Anna and I had gone to see them for the weekend, and the four of us plus, I think, Sarah and Andrew, who were very young at the time, were having lunch together in the kitchen. Mother was in full flow and Anna and I were listening politely when Dad said: "Maggie, Michael and Anna don't know these people and won't be interested in them." Mother went ballistic with him. I cannot remember what she said but it was spiteful, and I felt sorry for him. She could not abide any form of criticism, however mild.

There was a similar earlier incident over lunch at their house. This was the occasion when Sarah, who was a toddler at the time, stayed with her grandparents for the weekend. My parents had just bought a new Toyota and my father asked me what I thought of it. I indicated that I was not a fan of Japanese cars. It was an honest response, albeit not tactful. My mother, however, reacted furiously. She ranted for several minutes and accused me, among other things, of being obsessed with my image. At the time I was driving a small BMW which was, by some way, the most expensive car I had owned. I was by then a junior partner in a large London law practice and, before purchasing the BMW, my father had suggested that I should buy a Jaguar. I have never, however, been a person who indulged in extravagant cars and so my mother's accusation was absurd if it related to my vehicle. She did not specify anything else to justify it. I believe it was simply anger at what she regarded as an implied criticism. Incidentally, my view of Japanese cars has changed radically since then and I have been driving them for the past 12 years or more.

It is possible that jealousy contributed to her outburst. She certainly exhibited jealousy in respect of her sister Eileen, and this seemed to worsen as she grew older. Moreover, Tom has told me that Ruth, his wife, thought that Mother was envious of both her sons. I am not sure. What I believe is unarguable, however, is that she was resentful of both her daughters-in-law.

I never understood why Mother was resentful of Eileen. She was far better off financially than Eileen; she had two sons, whereas Eileen had been unable to have children with her husband; and she enjoyed a much better standard of living than Eileen. My suspicion is that the problem originated in their childhood in Egypt when Eileen had been spoiled after damaging her kidneys. This jealousy had also been apparent to Angela who has recounted to me an incident that took place over 60 years ago. Angela and Roy were staying with us for a few weeks before completing a house move. During that period my parents took them out for dinner to a local restaurant. The conversation turned to Eileen, and Angela remarked that Eileen was very house-proud. She had said this in the context of being slightly critical of Eileen, possibly explaining why Eileen rarely invited their mother, Elsie, to her home. Unfortunately, my mother took it the wrong way and burst out: "I am sick of hearing about Eileen. She's no more house-proud than I am." Angela recalled that she, Roy and my father were all embarrassed by this. I suspect it did not enhance the jollity of the evening.

Another example of my mother's hypersensitivity also occurred at the time that Angela and Roy were staying with us. Mother told me that Angela had come down one morning to say that there was no hot water for her bath. There were six of us then living in the house, and presumably the hot water tank had been emptied by the time she came to draw her bath. For a normal person this was not something that would cause offence or remain in the memory. It must have greatly annoyed Mother, however, as she told me about it several times over the years. I suppose she regarded Angela's comment as an implied criticism. It would, of course, have been nothing of the sort. My mother not only took offence very easily, she would also bear grudges forever.

My father died in 1984 at the age of 82. My mother was then aged 60. Bearing in mind that Dad had not enjoyed robust health (he had suffered from asthma, eczema and stomach ulcers prior to the arteriosclerosis), she was fortunate not to have been widowed even earlier. They had been married for 39 years.

Was the marriage a happy one? My father was frequently affectionate towards my mother and I remember that, when watching the television together in their adjoining armchairs, they would often hold hands. I do not remember her initiating any gestures of affection towards him. This might have been due to her somewhat reserved disposition. He would occasionally say to Tom and me: "I hope that when you boys get married, you will be even half as happy as your mother and me." This seems to me to have been a strange thing to say to your children. If you are happy, it should go without saying. I do, however, think that he was happy in the marriage.

My mother used to tell her family that Maurice was a good husband and that she was very happy. They, however, harboured doubts about that. I share those doubts. It could be a case of 'The lady doth protest too much.' It is true that my father was a loving and generous husband, but he was manifestly a poor husband in other ways. He was certainly a difficult man to live with. Mum used to get depressed at times, and this could last for several days. I suspect that he was the main cause of this.

Looking back on my parents' lives together, it is interesting to see how the dynamics changed. My father's domestic incompetence and laziness meant that he became increasingly dependent on my mother: domestically, in one of the businesses, as a chauffeuse and, ultimately, when he was an invalid, in almost every respect. She grew more confident and assertive, and developed a high self-regard, possibly fed by the praise lavished on her by her husband. I think it was such that she would never admit that her marriage was anything less than very happy.

It possible that the marriage was at its happiest after the move to East Sussex. By then my father was free of business worries and was mellowing with age. He was also free of his sons, so that he had his wife all to himself. My mother may have looked back at that period of contentment and blanked out all the difficulties that had preceded it.

Chapter Three
Maggie

My father died on a Sunday. Within a few hours of learning of his death, Anna and I drove down to East Sussex to be with Mother having first arranged for the children to be looked after at home. We stayed with her for a day or two before I had to return to work, having only just joined a new partnership. Anna either stayed on, or went back during the week, to help Mother in registering the death and making the funeral arrangements. The funeral itself was a particularly miserable affair. Mother did not want anyone, other than Tom and me and our wives, to attend and so nobody else was invited. As it was, Tom and his wife, Ruth, only turned up with a minute or so to spare.

Mother led a rather solitary existence for about a year after my father's death. She was almost a two-hour drive away from me and even more from Tom. Although she had several friends locally, I suspect that she did not see much of them during that time. Anna and I saw quite a lot of her. We would either go to stay with her for the weekend with the children, or she would come to us. We also started to take her away with us on our summer holidays and this continued for ten years or so. Tom did the same.

After a year Mother embarked on a small business venture. She had long had an interest in antique furniture and furnishings, and she came to an arrangement with a local antique business. She agreed to work in the shop for three days a week and, in lieu of a salary, the owners allowed her to use a corner of the premises to sell her own stuff. She began by selling things from her home that she no longer wanted, but then branched out into selling items she had purchased from third parties, often at local auctions. This was all on a small scale, but it was very beneficial for her; she got out and about and met lots of people.

Unfortunately, my mother's new pursuit did not result in her being any the less boring in her conversation. She would come to stay with us for the weekend and commence a virtual monologue from the moment she arrived in mid-afternoon on Friday. Unless it was during the school holidays, Anna would be on her own in the house when Mother arrived and would be the sole recipient of her 'news.' Anna would then go out in her car to collect Sarah and Andrew from their respective schools. When the children got home, Mother would repeat, for their benefit, either singly or together, what she had already told Anna. I would return from work at about 7:30 and Mother would start again. As we all tended to gather in the kitchen, by then Anna would have heard the same things three or four times. Mother would then hold forth over the evening meal. She showed little or no interest in what the rest of us had been doing. I think that grandparents instinctively know when it is time to withdraw from the centre of the stage and allow their children and grandchildren to have their share of the spotlight. Not my mother. She always had to be the centre of attention.

If I had not seen Mother for a few weeks, I used to look forward to seeing her in those days. Although I was aware of her shortcomings she was, nevertheless, my mother and there was still a deep (although somewhat diminished) well of affection from which she could draw. It was, I suppose, an example of the triumph of hope over experience as, after about 20 minutes of her solipsism, I began to worry about how we would cope for the rest of the weekend. In time we developed a system of dealing with her. I would sit with her in the lounge and, after a while, would be relieved by Anna or one of the children; then they, in turn, would be relieved by another of us, and so on.

Mother's antiques dealings were a pet topic of her conversation, although I think she spared the children the details of them. She would bring a little notebook with her and would go through, item by item, what she had bought and sold, and the sums involved. Although Anna and I were pleased that she now had this interest, hearing about it in such detail was tedious. The production of the dreaded notebook resulted in mutual glances, raised eyebrows and shifting of brains out of gear into neutral.

Tom's wife is an Israeli and he had converted to Judaism. As she does not celebrate Christmas, this enabled them to avoid having Mother stay with them over the holiday period. Consequently, she was always with us at Christmas and it was something that Anna used to dread. She was the one my mother tended to talk to the most, and this would be very testing when Anna was busy trying to prepare meals. It would be one of my jobs to sit with my mother in the lounge and listen to her while Anna worked in the kitchen. So, what should have been a joyous time for the family was somewhat marred by Mother's almost constant chatter. Anna and I felt sorry for the children, but they were fine about it. It was something they were used to. As she was their only living grandparent, they had no one to compare her with.

For our main holiday I used to rent a house with a swimming pool, in various parts of southern France or in the Algarve. I look back very fondly on those holidays. Andrew and I would be the first up, and we would go to the local village to buy a baguette and croissants for breakfast. Sometimes the whole family would go to the village later in the morning to buy provisions. We would play Trivial Pursuit or another game before lunch and would spend the rest of the day swimming, reading or just relaxing. Occasionally we would venture out to visit a nearby town of interest. In the evening we would eat out in local restaurants. This was the type of holiday on which we took Mother. We also took her with us to the USA on two occasions. On every holiday I paid for the entire cost of her travel, her accommodation and her meals, although I think she may have paid for one or two dinners each holiday as a gesture of thanks.

Mother came away with us for many years until she threw one of her tantrums on holiday in France. We had been out in the morning and Sarah had been rude to me. I told her off, but Anna said nothing. My mother let it be known that she thought this was wrong, but Anna declined to discuss it. This seemed to put Mother into a bad mood. When we got back to the house I told Anna that I thought she should have supported me; she explained that she would speak to Sarah in private as she wished to avoid a scene in front of the rest of the family. I informed my mother of this, but she remained tetchy. Later, over lunch, the subject of education arose. In this context I recalled that I had hated my school and felt that I would have been happier going to the local grammar school. This was a view that Mother had heard before and I think that, if she had been honest, she would probably have agreed with. On this occasion, however, she reacted very badly, saying that she and my father had made financial sacrifices to educate me privately, and that I was ungrateful. She worked herself up into a lather and retired upstairs to her bedroom. After a while Anna suggested that I should try to pacify her, so I went up to her room. She appeared to be as upset with Anna as she was with me. She said that Anna was a cold fish; I responded that Anna was the nicest person I had ever met. She said that I was a good husband, but I was not a good son. This was especially rich in the context of her being on holiday entirely at my expense. I ended up apologising for upsetting her and saying that it had not been my intention to do so. I asked her to come downstairs, which she eventually did. There was no apology from her for her tantrum, but that was not unusual. She would never admit to being in the wrong. That was the last occasion that I took her away on a family holiday.

It think it was after that holiday that Mother informed Tom that Anna and I had quarrelled, and she thought our marriage was in trouble. It was just silly gossip, and probably malicious too.

Tom was also a solicitor and had operated as a sole practitioner for several years before employing a full-time assistant. He eventually merged his practice with a larger one and took a 12-month sabbatical. He and his family based themselves in Israel and, from there, travelled to various destinations, including Australia. He took Mother with him for several months. He recalled that not once during that time did she offer to babysit the children so that he and Ruth could have an evening out on their own. I would have found that surprising but for the fact that she had only looked after our children on one evening during all the years when I had taken her away, and that was when Anna had been caring for Sarah all day when Sarah had been unwell.

Mother continued living in East Sussex for about 15 years after my father's death. After that time, she found it too tiring to drive from her home to Tom's home in North London. She wanted to move nearer to me, as that would greatly reduce the length of her journey to Tom; alternatively, she would have been content to live in another area in the southeast provided it had a railway station. She contacted various estate agents, as did Anna and I, and she had a considerable number of property particulars to consider. The process of finding a suitable property took many months. She would come to stay with us for several days at a time, and either I (at weekends) or Anna (on weekdays) would accompany her on viewings. Eventually she chose a house in Hampshire, close to the border with Surrey. This was about a 35-minute drive from us but in other respects it was far from ideal. Unlike her two previous houses it was only about 30 years old and was lacking in character; although it was in a village, the house itself was in quite a heavily-developed area and it did not enjoy any rural views; there was only one shop within walking distance; the nearest station was several miles away; it had a steep staircase; and, in the view of the other members of the family, it was too big. We had thought that Mother would move to an attractive cottage with two or three bedrooms and a couple of receptions. This house had four bedrooms, four reception rooms and two bathrooms. The total plot was about a quarter of an acre in size. When Anna and I asked why she needed such a large house, she said that it was to hold all her furniture. She would not entertain the thought of disposing of any of it as "my furniture is my life." Possibly a revealing statement, coming from a woman who had two children and six grandchildren.

Mother appeared generally content with her new house. If, on occasion, she found fault with something about it, she would let it be known that Anna had chosen it for her. This was typical of my mother. It was also untrue. Anna had provided her with the property particulars and had accompanied her to the viewing but had certainly not persuaded her to buy it.

After being in the house for a few months, my mother threw a party for her old friends from East Sussex. I think the current neighbours on either side were also invited. By that time, she had begun to suffer from hearing loss, and this caused an amusing incident at the party. My brother was present and there was another guest with the same name. This man said something to her when she had her back to him, but she had not heard him. I told her that Tom was speaking to her and, thinking that I was referring to my brother, she turned around with a "Yes, darling?" only to be facing the wrong Tom.

At some stage my mother was prescribed hearing aids. I think this was before she had left East Sussex. Unfortunately, she was too vain to wear them in public and failed to see the need to wear them at home. This was silly as her hair was sufficiently long to have hidden them. She would not accept that she was going deaf, insisting that she was just 'hard of hearing,' as if that were different. Shortly after moving to Hampshire, without consulting either me or Tom, she bought a single hearing aid of the type that fits inside the ear. This was from a private supplier and was not available from the National Health Service. It cost her about £1,000 and proved to be a waste of money as she barely ever wore it. She complained that it was too uncomfortable but failed to report this to the seller. I don't think she wore it sufficiently often to get used to it.

Mother's vanity was not confined to her hearing. To make herself appear taller she wore very high heels. I do not criticise that as such, but she did it to excess. She would even wear high heels indoors, albeit not stilettos. This continued into old age when at times she would struggle to walk unaided. Furthermore, the shoes she wore were fashionably narrow so that she ended up with deformed feet.

There was also a time after Mother had moved to Hampshire that she became convinced that a neighbour fancied her. She was in her early eighties at the time and, although she looked remarkably good for her age, was hardly a *femme fatale*. The man in question had done a small gardening job for her and, from my mother's account, I got the impression that he was probably a bit simple and over-talkative. She was convinced, however, that "he is after me."

Another of my mother's less than endearing traits was to find fault in people very easily and criticise them behind their backs, often for the most trivial of reasons. Moreover, once she had found grounds for criticism she would rarely forget them. Neither family nor friends were exempt. Her remark about Anna being 'a cold fish' was repeated numerous times to Tom and Ruth. Her criticisms of Ruth were legion. One of her female friends in East Sussex began to suffer the effects of old age but, instead of being understanding, Mother took the view that she was merely feeble and idle. She went on a cruise with another friend, also a widow, and later complained that the woman was a bore in the evenings, wanting to retire to bed early. It later emerged that the poor lady was very ill, and she died not long afterwards. Mother also formed a dislike of the couple (particularly the husband) who lived next door to her in Hampshire. Anna, Tom and I always found them pleasant and helpful.

As I grew older it became increasingly apparent that my brother was my mother's favourite, and that this had possibly been the case from an early stage. Whilst this was hurtful, it has not affected my relationship with my brother with whom I have always been close. I can understand why my mother favoured Tom. I think it was partly because he was much more reluctant than me to say something with which she disagreed. He would also occasionally confide in her (which was unwise as she was a gossip), whereas I had ceased to do so, certainly since getting married.

I have already mentioned the matter of the portraits, although I think that was more likely to have been my father's decision. A further instance was when I was in the upper fifth form at school. I had complained for years about school lunches, which were genuinely unpleasant, yet Mum refused to let me take a packed lunch. When Tom started complaining, however, she gave way, so I was able to have a packed lunch too.

There was the occasion when my parents were angry after I took the double bed from the Finchley flat, believing that I should have left that for Tom, even though he had retained all the other items of furniture. As a corollary to this, I was surprised, some years later, to learn that, when my parents moved to their smaller house in East Sussex, my mother had given Tom several pieces of furniture, including a small free-standing wardrobe which had been in my bedroom at home for most of my childhood. I had always been fond of that piece and was disappointed that it had not even been offered to me. The only piece of furniture she ever gave to Anna and me was a chest of drawers she no longer wanted. Some years later she took it back and replaced it with what was little more than an item of junk that we neither wanted nor needed.

The favouritism did not just apply to Tom and me; it also applied to our families. On her visits to us she would talk a lot about Tom's children but showed little interest in Sarah or

Andrew. This was more apparent as the children grew older. It even extended to our dogs. We had a much-loved German short-haired pointer which Mother tolerated and occasionally complained about. Some years later Tom bought a labradoodle, about which she was never less than complimentary.

My mother was always far more interested in Tom's career than mine. I put this down partly to the fact that he had been a sole practitioner from an early stage whereas I had been in partnership, a concept which she did not appear to understand. She seemed unable to recognise the difference between a profit-sharing partner and a salaried employee. Tom was conscious of Mother's lack of interest in my career and showed her, on one occasion, a copy of one of the two principal professional directories which referred to me as one of the leading practitioners in my field. It made no difference. Indeed, she never appeared able to remember the area of law in which I specialised.

My mother not only had favourites, she made it obvious to other people. She seemed to think that it was natural. I remember her asking a woman who her favourite child (or grandchild) was. Anna has never given any indication of having a favourite child and she would never gossip about Sarah or Andrew.

I cannot remember a single occasion when Mother telephoned to enquire as to my health or that of my family. This was not, however, another demonstration of favouritism, since Tom told me that she was the same with him. It was more likely an example of self-absorption.

Chapter Four

Eileen

Although I did not see a great deal of my aunt Eileen during my childhood, particularly after we moved to Kent, I was always rather fond of her. She was about the same height as my mother, although she looked smaller as she did not wear such high heels. Mother, moreover, had good posture whereas Eileen did not and, as she grew older, she became quite hunched. Like her older sister she was excessively talkative. She laughed a lot more than Mother, and she was younger in her attitudes.

As a young woman, Eileen had had a relationship with a man who got her pregnant and then abandoned her. She had, apparently with her mother's knowledge, an illegal abortion. This was a taboo subject within the family, and it seems that neither Eileen nor her mother ever discussed it with the other three sisters.

At the age of 22, Eileen met Bob Morris, who was five years her senior. After a courtship of three years, they married in 1950. I remember attending the wedding, possibly as a pageboy.

Bob came from a local family and had two brothers. I think he worked for a long while as a warehouse manager at Heathrow Airport. He was a quiet man by nature which was probably just as well, as life could have been very frustrating with a wife who talked incessantly. He was a solid character of whom Anna and I, and our children, were fond.

Eileen and Bob were unable to have children. It was suspected by her sisters that this may have been because of the abortion.

They led a quiet life, in a bungalow in semi-rural Middlesex, and I think their social life tended to be spent with Bob's brothers, and their wives, at the local pub. Eileen herself was not a social animal and I can only recall her having one other close female friend. That friendship did not endure for very long as the friend, who was a single woman, emigrated to Australia. Although Eileen had lived next door to the same couple for many years, they always addressed each other formally, never using first names.

Eileen was a nervous and timid woman. She had a habit, particularly as she grew older, of wringing her hands. Although Bob owned a car, Eileen never learned to drive. Because he worked for an airline, he was entitled to greatly discounted air travel and would have liked to take advantage of that. Unfortunately, Eileen was too nervous to fly. To the best of my knowledge, they only had one overseas holiday and that was in the Republic of Ireland.

According to my mother, Eileen and Bob had had separate bedrooms from an early stage of their marriage. Although Eileen was said to have been very house-proud in her younger days, this did not accord with my mother's account. She considered Eileen to be lazy and selfish. One story I recall is that when Eileen changed the beds, she gave herself fresh sheets and put one or both sheets from her bed onto Bob's.

Bob's two brothers, and I think the wife of one of them, pre-deceased him, and the other wife ended up in a care home suffering from dementia. After that Eileen and Bob's social activities presumably all but disappeared.

At some stage after my father died, Anna and I started inviting Eileen and Bob to spend Christmas Day or Boxing Day with us. We had bought Andrew a quarter-size snooker table as a Christmas present and he and Bob used to play several games together in the afternoon. I think Bob genuinely enjoyed playing, although there was the bonus of being able to escape to the playroom, thereby avoiding the constant chatter of my mother and Eileen.

Bob died in 1997. Mother went to stay with Eileen for a few days leading up to the funeral. She reported later that Eileen had very little food in the house and seemed content to live off tinned corned beef. Tom and I attended the funeral and the reception afterwards at Eileen's house. There was an incident there that Angela recalled many years later. I was telling her how Tom was very much our mother's favourite. Angela said that she had long been aware of that and mentioned how, at Bob's wake, Maggie had squeezed Tom's cheek, in front of others, saying "Isn't he lovely!" Angela had thought that that was a strange thing to do to a man in his late forties.

After Bob's death, Eileen seemed to have an almost hermit-like existence. The friend who had emigrated to Australia returned to the area to live with her sister, and Eileen saw them occasionally. Unfortunately, the friend became ill with dementia and I think the renewal of the friendship was short-lived.

Eileen had, I understand, long had a tendency to hypochondria. This became more apparent to me following Bob's death. Whenever I enquired as to her health, she would rarely, if ever, say that she was well. There was always something wrong with her, the general complaint being osteoporosis.

PART TWO

Chapter Five
2002

I retired at the end of April 2002, at the age of 55. This fulfilled an ambition for which I had planned for many years. As it transpired, it was fortunate for my mother that I had given up work as it was later that year that Anna and I first became aware that Mother's mental health was declining. She was then aged 78. Increasing deafness was also a problem.

Anna and I now think that we missed earlier signs of the dementia. About a couple of years beforehand, I had bought Anna a new set of saucepans as her Christmas present. (It is a source of amusement for me and our children how she almost always requests functional gifts.) Thereafter, every time Mother visited us, and was sitting in the kitchen while Anna was cooking, she would ask, "How are you getting on with your new saucepans, Anna?" This went on for a few years and Anna and I used to have a chuckle about it, although not in front of Mother who could not tolerate mirth at her expense.

It is common for elderly people to struggle with advances in technology. Tom and I had given our mother a video recorder several years beforehand, but she had never managed to operate it successfully, despite our efforts to teach her. We had also bought her a cordless telephone which she could take with her around the house so that, when the phone rang, she would not have to hurry to another room to answer it. It was apparent, however, that she was not using it as she would quite often fail to answer our calls. In early December 2002, I went to her house to try to deal with both problems. Unfortunately, I discovered that the video recorder was malfunctioning and, after talking to her about it, it was apparent that, even if the device could be repaired, it was probably not worth the cost of doing so as she was unlikely to use it. I also discovered that she had mislaid her cordless phone. After a lengthy search I managed to find it and set it up for her. That proved to be a wasted effort as it was clear from subsequent experiences that she barely ever used it.

Mother frequently boasted of how she had managed her financial affairs on her own after my father died, and the astuteness of her investment decisions. In reality, she was quite naïve in relation to investments, and those that she made were either on the advice of various brokers or as a result of her having seen advertisements in newspapers. In fact, two of her investments were poor and resulted in her losing a significant amount of capital. In 2002 I began to take over responsibility for her financial affairs and I asked my independent financial adviser to review her portfolio. As part of the review, Mother and I had a meeting at his office to which I took her up to London on the train. The meeting with the IFA was embarrassing as Mother kept prattling and looking for praise for her financial acumen. The meeting was taking far longer than needed but, when I tried tactfully to steer her back to relevant matters, she was rude to me, which was uncomfortable both for me and for the financial adviser. Another example of her thin skin.

As was the case every year, Mother came to stay with us over the Christmas period and, on 28th December, I made the following note in my diary:

Mother went home this morning. Anna and I have noticed a significant deterioration in her over the past 12 months. Her conversation is repetitive, and she appears not to remember things she has been told, sometimes even a few minutes later.

We did not know then just how much worse she would get.

CHAPTER SIX
2003

ON CHRISTMAS EVE, MY MOTHER AND I HAD BEEN having a chat on our own. She raised the subject of my relationship with my father, recalling that I had not got on with him very well. I thought we were having a frank conversation and made a comment to the effect that he was 'too bloody old' to have been the father of two young sons. It was heartfelt, but not tactful, and I regretted having said it when I thought about it later. She did not, however, react to it at the time and the subject was not brought up again over the holiday.

In mid-January, Anna and I flew from Heathrow at the start of a long visit to Australasia. The previous evening, I rang my mother to say goodbye and to reassure her that Tom would be seeing her regularly and would deal with any problems that arose. I was shocked by her hostility. She had clearly been dwelling on our conversation on Christmas Eve and I suspect that she had remembered the phrase I had used but forgotten the context. I was unable to placate her and did not want to be leaving on such bad terms. I rang Tom to inform him of the position and he agreed to try to sort things out.

Having been away for 11 weeks, I next saw my mother on Easter Sunday when she came for lunch and stayed the night. She appeared to have forgotten our falling out. In my diary I recorded:

Mother's short-term memory seemed worse than ever. She asked the same questions or made the same comments several times over.

There is another diary note on 9th November 2003 in which I mention the deterioration in my mother's short-term memory. Then, a few days later, it became apparent that her condition was even worse than I had realised.

Tom and I had been concerned that our mother was using a watering can to irrigate her garden. Although the garden was not large, it was still an onerous task for a woman of 79. We had therefore, as a Christmas or birthday present, had an automatic irrigation system installed. On 18th November, I had an appointment at my mother's house with the owner of the firm that had dealt with the installation. Mother had forgotten all about the appointment and was therefore surprised when I arrived. Whilst there, I learned that she had had a minor motor accident when driving back from my house the previous week. She was clearly upset by the incident and did not know what to do. She had, however, contacted her insurance brokers and had received an accident report form. She had also received a notice from the police, as she had failed to stop and provide information to the driver of the other vehicle. I completed the report form for her based on her very sketchy account of what had happened. She was so vague that it was unclear to me exactly where the accident had occurred. She maintained that it was entirely the fault of the other driver, a much younger woman, who had failed to stop at a red light. She also said that she had not stopped as that woman had driven away. I made a couple of telephone calls on her behalf and gave her detailed instructions on what to do. I possibly gave her a note of these so that she would remember.

The following day I received a telephone call from Mother. My diary note reads as follows:

She had apparently forgotten what I had told her yesterday and appeared rather confused. Hopefully this state of mind is the result of stress and is not a sign of dementia.

Despite explaining to her once again what she needed to do, the following day I had a further telephone call from her. She was still confused and could not understand why we needed to contact the police. She was also uncertain whether she had spoken to her motor insurers the day before, and so I had to ring them to obtain clarification of where things stood.

Over the next few days it became apparent that Mother's account of the accident was incorrect in almost every respect. The accident was not in the place I had understood it to have been, and it was almost certainly her fault. The other driver did not jump a traffic light, it was my mother who drove into her. Moreover, the other driver had stopped with a view to exchanging information, but my mother simply drove off. When I discussed all of this with Mother, she refused to accept that she was in any way to blame and was offended that I was dubious. Anyway, she stuck to her story and I drafted a letter for her to send to the police which seemed to do the trick. She was fortunate to escape prosecution.

*

During the evening of 14th December, I received a telephone call from my aunt Angela. She informed me that Eileen had been admitted to hospital with a urinary tract infection and in a confused state. As I was the relative who lived the closest to her, I offered to contact the hospital in the morning. I did so and was informed that she would be discharged in the late afternoon. I drove to the hospital, which is about 45 minutes away, and arrived at 2:30, only to find that Eileen had already been discharged. I therefore drove on to her house. She confirmed she had had an infection and had been diagnosed with 'heptatic confusion.' Tablets had been prescribed. She seemed no different to usual in that she wittered for an hour or so, mainly recounting tales from her past, with an emphasis on her childhood in Egypt. In nearly all of her conversations with me Eileen seemed to dwell on the past. It was as if nothing of substance in her life had occurred for the last 40 or 50 years.

When I got home, I looked up 'heptatic confusion' online but could find no such ailment. I think that the hospital had possibly formed a preliminary diagnosis of hepatic encephalopathy, which is a deterioration of brain function caused by liver disease. With the benefit of hindsight, I think the confusion may have been the first sign of dementia, although I understand that urinary tract infections can cause confusion in elderly patients.

On the evening of 17th December, Angela telephoned to report that Eileen's neighbour had contacted her to say that Eileen had been very confused that morning. The neighbour had been sufficiently concerned that she called for an ambulance to take Eileen to hospital. Eileen was discharged either later that day or the next morning. I contacted her GP and requested that he should examine her at her home. He did so, and I was told that he was arranging for blood tests the following day. Whether he did that, I do not know as I heard nothing further from him.

Eileen was again taken to hospital on 23rd December but was not admitted as an in-patient. I spoke to her at home later that day and she told me that she had again been suffering from 'heptatic confusion' and had been prescribed some different pills.

I think that Eileen spent Christmas with her late husband's nephew and his wife. My mother stayed with us as usual. On 27th December I took her, Sarah and Andrew to see Eileen. Mother had not seen her sister for a year or so and was shocked by how old she looked.

CHAPTER SEVEN

2004

IN 2004 I SAW MY MOTHER THREE OR FOUR TIMES A month, and Tom did likewise. Most times I would drive over to her house and stay for a light lunch. On other occasions, she would come to us in the afternoon, have an evening meal and stay the night.

In January, Tom and I hosted a large family dinner at a London restaurant in honour of our mother's 80th birthday. Anna and I, together with Sarah and Andrew, arrived at the appointed time and were followed shortly thereafter by Tom's children. We were offered a Prosecco and, rather foolishly, I accepted without having seen a wine list. Some of us had had three each before Mother arrived with Tom and Ruth, with whom she was staying for a few days, an hour late. Mother had thought that just the three of them were going out for a meal and so was greatly surprised to see the rest of us awaiting her arrival. It was an enjoyable evening, albeit tarnished by the size of the bill, of which the cost of the Proseccos was a significant element.

Tom recalls a grimly amusing incident that occurred while Mother was staying with him. It may have been at that time. They were watching a television news programme in which the news headlines were repeating on a scrolling bar at the bottom of the screen. Reference was made to either a disaster or terrorist attack somewhere in the world. Mother commented on it. When the headline was repeated about a minute later, she said, "Oh, my God. Not another one!"

At the end of April, I went to see my mother and it became apparent that she was confused over her investments. These, together with her State Pension, provided her only income; she had no private pension. I offered to sort out her paperwork and schedule the investments for her if she provided me with all the papers. A few days later, I collected a large amount of financial papers which I took home to incorporate into a filing system. They were in such a mess that it took me several days, over the course of about four weeks, to complete the job as best I could. There were all sorts of problems apart from the sheer volume of documents. She had made no attempt to keep them in chronological order, or even to separate one investment from another. Moreover, after dealing with the papers she had initially given me, and realising that various items were missing, I learned that she kept her papers in more than one place at home. She had forgotten that when providing me with the initial batch.

There were a variety of other difficulties. One example was where an investment company, with whom she had a personal equity plan (the predecessor of an individual savings account), had failed to make the last three payments when they fell due. I had picked this up from her bank statements. She was oblivious of the fact. A telephone call resolved the problem. The company had incorrect details of her address and had held back the payments after a cheque had been returned to it, thinking she had moved.

It had become apparent that, at some stage in the not too distant future, Mother would need to have a power of attorney in place. It was important for her to sign one while her mental capacity was such that she understood what she was doing. Fortunately, she was not resistant to signing the document, which she did in July.

Mother's hearing had deteriorated to the extent that she was occasionally not hearing the telephone ring, and so I ordered an amplified one for her. This was delivered in June and I set it up, programming in the numbers of the people she was most likely to call. Despite explaining several times how to use the automatic dialling procedure, she never got to grips with it.

When I went to see her a few days later, she was depressed and rather agitated. For possibly the first time she seemed to accept that she was becoming confused. This was a rare event; her high self-esteem precluded self-criticism. She had cheered up by the following week when Anna and I took her to lunch in her local pub.

When visiting her, I would often deal with her post and keep her filing up to date. She had reached the stage where she needed help with her domestic admin.

Another sign of decline was apparent at the end of August when Anna and I went to Mother's house for lunch. She had rearranged this from the previous day on the basis that she would have more time to do some cooking. We were therefore surprised to be served with cold meat and a plain salad. She had been a good cook and we therefore suspected that she was losing her confidence. Unfortunately, one of the few meals she had never excelled in producing was a salad. These had not changed since my childhood: tomatoes, lettuce and cucumber.

The huge variety of different salad ingredients available at the larger supermarkets had simply passed her by.

In late September, Anna and I took my mother away for a short break in Suffolk. The main purpose was for her to see a friend from the time when my parents, Tom, and I had lived in Kent. This old lady had moved to Suffolk to be near her daughter. I had booked us into a rather luxurious hotel for two nights and had told Mother that she would be able to wear some smart clothes there. This had been at Tom's prompting as we both knew how she liked to dress up given the opportunity which, by then, she rarely had. This backfired badly.

The break got off to a miserable start. Anna and I arrived at Mother's house to find her wearing a suit. When I complimented her on her appearance, she bit my head off, indicating that she had taken offence at my telling her to dress smartly and that she did not need to be instructed by me what to wear. Moreover, she said she would not have bothered if she had known what Anna (who was appropriately dressed for a long car journey) would be wearing. This was so gratuitously offensive, it was almost amusing. The strange thing was that she had not taken any offence at the time of our original conversation, so I do not think she had misconstrued what I had said; instead, she had misremembered it.

The situation was aggravated by the fact that she had drawn a large cheque in respect of a world cruise she had booked for January, without transferring the requisite funds from a building society account. This was despite my having explained to her what she had to do. Her oversight necessitated a journey of several miles to the building society, which was in the opposite direction to the one we would be taking to Suffolk. I was not best pleased by this but, instead of being contrite, which would have been out of character anyway, she appeared to be of the view that there was no need to visit the building society. She failed to appreciate that, without transferring the funds to her current account, her cheque would bounce.

On the way to Suffolk, we stopped for a light lunch at an historic hotel in Essex. After lunch we visited two National Trust properties. Mother did not seem interested in the second of these and stayed in the car while Anna and I had a quick look around.

We dined at the hotel on both evenings we were in Suffolk. Pre-dinner drinks in the bar on one of the evenings proved to be another disagreeable experience. Mother's hearing aid did not appear to be working and she had failed to bring any spare batteries with her. Being deaf, she tended to speak loudly, and this became potentially embarrassing when she began making critical comments about the appearance of other customers. I suggested politely that she should lower her voice at which she took offence and became unpleasant.

On the last day of our trip to Suffolk, we went to visit my mother's friend. The old lady was 92 at the time and, despite being frail, was noticeably more on the ball than Mother, who was 12 years her junior. Anna and I talked with the friend's daughter, leaving the two old ladies to chat together, albeit my mother monopolised the conversation. Because of her loud voice, we could not avoid being aware of a lot of what she was saying, which included her telling her friend that "Tom is so wealthy," in a way that clearly implied that I was the poor relation.

I had planned the short break carefully as a treat for my mother, and it was quite expensive. She demonstrated her appreciation by behaving throughout in an odious manner. Clearly her memory-related problems stemmed from her dementia, but her over-sensitivity and spitefulness were part of her character.

The well of affection for my mother had, by now, almost run dry.

Shortly after returning from the trip to Suffolk, Mother rang me to say that she could not find her coral necklace and thought she must have left it in her room at the hotel. She asked me to contact the hotel to ask if it had been found. Anna and I were familiar with the necklace as it had matching earrings. Neither of us could recall her wearing it whilst away. Nevertheless, I rang the hotel who informed me that no such jewellery had been handed in. On being told of this, Mother's immediate reaction was that the chambermaid must have stolen it. This incident foreshadowed a later, more serious incident.

*

In early December, Eileen moved from her bungalow to a flat in Kingsley Wood, a development of sheltered accommodation. Mother had stated the intention of helping her sister with the move; she would drive there the previous day and stay the night. I had expressed reservations about this as she had not driven on her own to Eileen's bungalow for several years, and I did not think she would be able to find her way. I doubt that she had ever been able to read a map. It, therefore, did not come as a surprise to me when she rang the following day to say that, after starting off, she had felt dizzy and had returned home. I agreed to go, the next day, in her place. When I rang Eileen to tell her, she was already in a nervous state.

I spent much of the following day, Tuesday, helping Eileen with her move. Fortunately, the removal men were patient, as she was flustered and dithering. I was quite shocked at the extent of her mental decline as she appeared to have little short-term memory.

I spent Wednesday at Eileen's new flat helping her to unpack. It was a trying experience. On Thursday, Anna came with me to continue the unpacking and to help arrange the furniture.

*

On Friday, having spent three days with my aunt, it was my mother's turn to try my patience. She was due to embark on her cruise in January and needed to have several items of clothing altered. She had learned of a dressmaker, who lived in a village about a 30-minute drive away, and I had agreed to take her there. She said she knew a route that was better than the one I had proposed taking and, fool that I was, I followed her directions. We got lost and arrived 25 minutes late for her appointment. To make matters worse, Mother maintained that it was not her fault. Nothing ever was.

On the way back we followed my route, which took about half as long as the outward journey. My mother spent much of the time conducting a character assassination of Eileen. She was frequently critical of her sister and, while some of what she said was justified, the depth of ill-feeling was something I did not understand, especially as I never heard Eileen say anything unpleasant about my mother. In an attempt to change the subject, I tried telling her about my recent holiday, but she evinced little interest in it. After we arrived back at her house, she wanted to show me the itinerary for her cruise and seemed surprised that I had already seen it. In fact, she had shown it to me on several of my visits.

*

The following Tuesday I was back at Eileen's and was surprised to see that she had made little or no effort to unpack during the four days since my previous visit. One of my mother's complaints about Eileen was her laziness. It seemed to be justified. I spent five hours with her that day and completed emptying the boxes as well as dealing with some of her post. Four days later, I returned to do a few more jobs, including hanging some of her pictures.

*

The Christmas period was particularly stressful.

On 23rd December I drove to my mother's to take her to her dressmaker. I arrived there at about 12:30 but she had not returned from the hairdresser by then. She went to the hairdresser once a week and never washed her own hair. I believe this was not uncommon with women of her generation. I had a set of two keys for her house, one for a Yale lock and one for a deadlock. As far as I can recall, I had not had to use them before as she had always been at home when I called. I was unable to get in the front door because the Yale key did not appear to fit. I did, however, manage to enter via the back door using only the deadlock key as the Yale lock on that door had not engaged. When, however, I went out to try the front door again, and shut the back door, the Yale lock did engage, and I was locked out! When my mother returned, I explained what had happened. She then used her set of keys, but with no success. We were both locked out! We went round to the next-door neighbours, who were about to start their lunch, and called a locksmith from their telephone. (I was frequently guilty in those days, and still am to a lesser extent, of forgetting to take my mobile with me when I left home.) We were there for over two hours before he came. It was an uncomfortable wait as my mother was in a bad mood and was very truculent with me, much to the discomfort of the neighbours. When the locksmith eventually arrived, he discovered that the same key fitted both locks on the front door which, he said, was unusual. Although I had tried the same key in both locks, it had not worked on one of them because, according to the locksmith, the lock had grit in it. I had not persevered. It was all rather embarrassing. By the time we got into the house, it was too late to go to the dressmaker. When I asked my mother why she had not explained to me that the same key operated both locks, she said she had forgotten. She did not apologise for this or for wasting several hours of my time.

I was unable to take Mother to the dressmaker the following day, Christmas Eve, but she said that she would be able to find her own way. She arranged to call there in the early afternoon and would then get to our house before dark. She had not arrived by 5:00 pm and was not answering her phone. I rang the dressmaker and was informed that she had arrived about an hour and a half late and had left some time ago. I eventually managed to contact her on the telephone. By this time, it was very dark, and she seemed a little flustered. Sarah and Andrew, who were home for Christmas, kindly drove over to collect her. It was apparent that she had got lost both on the way to the dressmaker and on the way back, but she would not admit to it.

For the second Christmas in succession, Mother forgot to bring either of her hearing aids with her. This meant that, when we watched the television, the volume had to be unpleasantly high.

On Christmas morning I took my mother with me to collect Eileen from her new flat. The two of them sat together in the back of the car, on the return journey, and talked together non-stop for the whole of the 35-minute journey. They continued this incessant chatter all day, until Eileen left our house just after 9:30 that evening. I had arranged for a taxi to take her home. It was amusing in that they appeared at times to be having parallel conversations which bore little or no relevance to what the other was saying. It was possibly a case of Eileen not being interested in what Mother had to say, and Mother not hearing what Eileen was saying. For both of them, talking was the principal element of conversation; listening was of little importance. Fortunately, they were talking mainly to each other. This meant that the rest of us were able to converse among ourselves and enjoy our day.

Anna drove Mother home on 27th December. Sarah observed that her grandmother's mental state was worse than ever.

CHAPTER EIGHT

2005

JUST HOW BAD MY MOTHER HAD BECOME WAS EVEN more apparent about a fortnight later when Anna and I went to collect her to drive her to Southampton for the start of her cruise. We arrived at her house just after 11:00 am. She told us she had finished packing and just needed us to take her three suitcases downstairs. She said she would make us lunch before we set off. Embarkation was due to commence at 2:00 pm, with the ship leaving port two hours later. I wanted to arrive before 2:00 to avoid her having to endure a lengthy queue. In the event we did not set off until 1:15 and did not arrive until 2:40, by which time the queue was very long.

The delay was entirely down to my mother who was at her confused worst. Firstly, she insisted that the same key fitted the padlock on each of her three cases, when it clearly did not. We eventually found the other two keys in her handbag. Then she could not find a hearing aid. After spending a long time looking for it, Anna discovered it in the hand luggage. During that search, Mother realised that she had not packed any shoes.

They had to go in a separate bag. By this time, it was too late to have lunch at the house and so Anna made sandwiches to eat *en route*. While she was doing that, I put the cases in the car, only to discover later that Mother had left several items of clothing on a bed in a guest room. The cases had to be removed from the car and Anna had to find room in one of them to accommodate the additional items. By this time, we were both stressed out.

On the way to Southampton, I commented on how much later we were than I had planned, to which my mother responded, "Well, you should have left earlier." So, as usual, it was someone else's fault. There was, however, the major consolation that she would be away for almost 12 weeks.

Anna, Tom and I had all had misgivings about Mother going on such a long cruise. Her behaviour on the day of departure did nothing to reassure us.

During her absence, I called in at my mother's house on a weekly basis to check that everything was in order, water the houseplants and collect the mail. In addition, I discovered a lot more of her papers which I took home. Anything that needed to be retained I put in the filing system that I had started for her. While doing this I discovered that, for the past two years, she had been paying two different companies to service her boiler and central heating. Shortly before her return, Anna and I cleaned her house.

*

During March, Eileen contacted me to say that the financial advisers at her bank had been in touch with a view to arranging an appointment. I agreed to accompany her to this meeting, which took place at the bank's local branch. I think it was on that occasion that the bank suggested that Eileen ought to grant me a power of attorney. I agreed to act as such, but only on the basis that I did so jointly with someone else. This was because I wished to avoid any subsequent suggestion that I had acted improperly. I therefore spoke to her nephew on her late husband's side, with whom she occasionally spent Christmas Day, and he agreed to act with me. I then prepared an enduring power and took it with me when I went to see her a month later. I left it with her, together with an explanatory booklet, so that she could consider it at her leisure.

*

At the end of March, I drove down to Southampton with Tom to collect Mother from her cruise. She appeared to have had a good time, but her memory had certainly not improved. She came ashore with only two suitcases. Fortunately, I remembered that she had taken away three and Tom was able to retrieve the missing one from her cabin. I suspect she had a lot of difficulty in finding her way around a large cruise ship and that she needed considerable help.

She had bought items of clothing, from the boutique on the ship, for all members of the family. Sadly, it was unlikely any of us would want to wear them. She treated Tom and me to lunch at the local pub and we chatted about her holiday. She seemed unable to recall much about where she had been and, when I asked whether she had taken many photographs, she said that she had not taken any because her camera was not working. I thought that she had simply forgotten how to operate it. Moreover, she could easily have purchased another one on her travels. She said that she was not bothered about the lack of photos to remind her of her holiday as, pointing to her head, she told us "It's all up there." Sadly, very little of it was up there.

About a week later, I spent almost five and a half hours at my mother's, dealing with various matters on her behalf, including renewing her medical insurance but with a different insurer. I also discovered that she had changed her energy supplier but appeared to have no recollection of having done so. It seemed, from the correspondence, that the change had been made because of a cold call, either in person or by telephone. I cancelled the new contract.

The following week I spent almost four hours with Mother, dealing principally with several financial matters, including helping her to change the pin number for her debit card to one she might be better able to remember.

In early May, my mother came to us in the late afternoon and to have dinner. She stayed the night. She was still capable of driving to places she was used to visiting.

In June, Mother's accountant contacted her to arrange to call at her home to go through her papers in order to prepare her annual claim for repayment of tax deducted at source from her savings. As she now knew very little about her investments, I suggested to her that I should be present, and she agreed to liaise with me over a date. She forgot to do so, and, in the event, I had to go there at very short notice. The meeting took place in mid-June and I arrived at her house shortly before 2:30 pm, the agreed time. She told me that I was early as the accountant was not due until 4:00. She had, moreover, forgotten that she had fixed the time and date and thought that I had done so. As it happened, the accountant arrived about 15 minutes after me. During that visit, I found that Mother had been retaining a lot of her post and other papers instead of giving them to me to deal with. As a consequence, I again had a backlog of papers to handle.

It was very difficult for me to deal with my mother's affairs at that time. Whilst she was happy for me to take over the administrative burden, she did not accept that she needed help and would occasionally do things of her own volition without letting me know. This could be exasperating, but to put the power of attorney into operation was out of the question; she would not even have entertained the possibility. She seemed to be in a state of denial of her mental decline and was occasionally resentful of my involvement, appearing to regard it as unnecessary interference.

I have recently been advised by the Alzheimer's Society that it is not uncommon for a person with dementia to be in denial, although it is hard to know whether the person is in denial or is experiencing lack of insight. The latter is related to loss of activity in specific areas in the front of the brain and results in the person with dementia being unable to recognise – and therefore acknowledge – changes in their behaviour and personality.

Another example of my mother's inability to manage her affairs was apparent from a visit I made in mid-June. One of the matters we had discussed, following her return from the cruise, was the duplication of boiler maintenance contracts. With her knowledge, I cancelled one of them but, on the visit in question, I learned that she had taken out a new contract with the same service company. Moreover, she had posted direct debit mandates in respect of that contract on successive days. I therefore had to cancel the new contract.

*

Eileen had her 80th birthday in August and, to celebrate the occasion, Anna and I took her out for Sunday lunch at a restaurant. Although she gave her jaws a thorough workout, this was in talking rather than eating. We were rather shocked at her tiny appetite. When we got back to her flat, Eileen and I signed her power of attorney, with her friend from the other flat on her floor witnessing our signatures. The other nephew signed a few days later.

*

Following one of my regular visits to my mother, I made a note in my diary, on 17th September:

It is becoming increasingly apparent that, without me keeping an eye on her, she would overlook a lot of things.

Shortly afterwards Anna and I went on holiday. Five days after returning, I went to see Mother and my diary note of the visit reads:

She seems to have deteriorated since I last saw her in that her medium-term memory is now erratic.

Hitherto the memory loss was only apparent regarding her short-term memory.

I continued to see Mother every week or so and there were no more major incidents until Christmas, although I did return home on occasions feeling stressed.

During the afternoon of 24th December my mother missed the turn-off on the A3, when driving to us for Christmas. She did not know where she was and pulled into a lay-by, where she asked someone for help. This man rang me on his mobile and explained what had happened. Anna and I had to drive out to the A3 to find my mother who was waiting for us in the lay-by. I then drove her to our house in her car and Anna drove ours home.

That evening Mother and I watched a film on the television, but she gave up after a while and went to bed early. I think she had difficulty in following it.

On Christmas morning, I went with Andrew in the car to collect Eileen. She talked the entire way home, and she and Mother then had one of their talkathons for the rest of the day, until Eileen was taken home by taxi at about 7:30 pm. Mother was worried by the weather forecast on Boxing Day, fearing that she might have to drive back in snow or icy conditions. She therefore decided to cut short her stay by returning that afternoon. Over lunch that day she was particularly repetitive, asking the same questions over and over again. Anna and I were concerned that she might get lost again on the way home and so I drove Mother in her car, following Anna in hers, to a turn-off on the A3. All she had to do from there was to go straight ahead at a roundabout and follow the signs. Unfortunately, even that was beyond her, and she got lost.

Chapter Nine
2006

Tom, Anna and I had all been worried for a while about Mother continuing to drive. We felt that she might be a danger to herself and to others. At the beginning of January, Anna and I went to see her to discuss our concerns. She made it clear, in an aggressive manner, that she was not prepared to give up her car as she felt that, by doing so, she would lose her independence. She did, however, indicate that she would only drive locally.

By this time almost every visit to my mother was proving to be a stressful experience. She was by nature very talkative, but now she was also repetitive and deaf. She would ask a question, I would answer it and would often have to repeat my answer because she had not heard it. She would then ask the same question, or make the same point, every few minutes. She also went through a spell of reading aloud to me something she had found interesting in her newspaper. She proceeded to another item on the same page, followed by a third. She then started again with the first piece. The repetition was, of course, a consequence of her loss of short-term memory, and I just had to be patient. She could not help her dementia, but she could have done something about the deafness. Whenever I asked her why she was not wearing a hearing aid she would respond: "I don't need to because I don't see anybody." I would reply "You're seeing me," but that made no difference.

To reduce the stress, Tom and I decided to visit her less often. Instead of each of us going every week, we would visit on alternate weeks. This meant that she would see at least one of us once a week, and my son and daughter also visited her occasionally with their respective partners. Quite often, when visiting, Tom or I would take her out for lunch. The reduced number of visits only lasted a few months; after that her deteriorating condition necessitated the resumption of weekly visits.

On a visit I made in mid-February, I attempted to evaluate Mother's short-term memory with a simple test I had heard about. I gave her three objects to remember and, 15 minutes later, I asked her to recall them. Not only had she forgotten the objects, she had also forgotten that I had set a test.

I think it was around this time that my mother had a visit from an Australian couple she had met on her cruise. They were touring the UK, seeing friends and relations. They had contacted Mother and it was arranged that they would come to see her and stay for the night. She had told me about this couple on her return from the cruise and had been singing their praises. This view changed following their visit. It appears that, during the night, the husband moved into one of the other bedrooms (where, fortunately, the bed had been made up), presumably because he had been unable to sleep. According to my mother, she had not discovered this until after they had gone. She was very annoyed by it, thought their behaviour was disgraceful and banged on about it for a few weeks. I think it is unlikely she was not told that a second bed had been used but, even if she had not, her reaction was excessive, especially regarding people who had been kind to her on the ship.

In mid-March came a traumatic event that had significant repercussions for my mother, and for me. I rang her on a Thursday evening to let her know that I would be round the following day to see her. She told me that she had had a funny turn in her car the previous Saturday. In those days she would drive to a town about four miles away, on a Saturday morning, to visit the hairdresser and then on to Sainsbury's to do her supermarket shopping. She said she had felt faint and had pulled up at the side of the road. She remembered having a terrible pain in her head. (I wondered later if she had had a mini-stroke.) A man then drove her home in her car. I asked her whether she had seen her doctor about the incident, but she said that she had not as she had felt nervous about driving.

The next day I made an appointment for my mother to see her doctor that afternoon. I spoke to the GP and explained what had happened. I also said that my brother and I were worried about Mother's fitness to drive and asked the GP to attempt to assess this. At the appointment, at which I was also present, the doctor advised her against driving in the future. Mother indicated that she did not accept this advice. When it was put to her that she might be the cause of an accident, she shrugged it off on the basis that, if she were killed, she would not know anything about it. She did not appear to have considered that she might be the cause of someone else being killed or injured. She was given a memory test which revealed clear problems with her short-term memory. The GP said that she would arrange for a colleague, specialising in memory problems, to see my mother at home.

The man who had driven my mother home on Saturday had left her with a note of his name and telephone number. I rang him that evening to thank him for his help. I then learned that the circumstances were very different from what had been described by Mother. My letter to her GP of the following day shows just how serious her condition had become.

I am grateful to you for seeing my mother at short notice yesterday. Her short-term memory is such that, on emerging from the surgery, she expressed the view that you had not found much wrong with her and it appeared that she had forgotten the advice you gave her about giving up driving.

Unfortunately, it is now apparent that the situation last Saturday is far more serious than we had been led to believe. I was able to speak yesterday evening to Paul, the man who drove my mother home. He informed me that the incident occurred at about midnight. He lives about two miles from my mother's house and had just left home to collect his daughter who had been out for the evening. My mother's car was stationary, on his road, with its lights on, and was blocking the road. He got out to investigate and spoke to my mother who seemed very tired and somewhat distressed. She said she could not find her way home, although she could remember her address. It seems that he drew her a sketch map but, as she still seemed vague, he had to drive her home himself in her car. His wife went to collect the daughter. On arriving at her house, there was a problem in gaining entry. I have had a similar problem with her myself when she became confused with her door keys. The poor chap either did not leave until 1:00 am or did not get home until that time. He was sufficiently concerned about her that he went to see her the next day. She told him that she would not tell me about the incident. At some stage (and I am unsure whether this was at night or when he saw her the following morning) she remembered that her shopping from Sainsbury's was in the boot of her car.

After speaking to Paul, I rang my mother who denied that this had happened at night yet later recalled Paul saying that it was 'nearly midnight.' I ascertained that her hairdressing appointment had been at 1:00 pm on Saturday and would have lasted for about one and a half hours, after which she went to the supermarket for a similar period. When I asked her what she had been doing for the next eight hours she was unable to explain but kept insisting that she had pulled up on a grass verge at the side of the road as she was feeling faint and that was where Paul had found her. I did not pursue the matter further as she was becoming angry with me.

I fear that what may have happened is that, after pulling up, my mother either blacked out or fell asleep and remained where she was for several hours. When she set off again, she was confused and did not know where she was. I cannot tell whether she is now being deliberately evasive or simply cannot remember what happened. I suspect it is the latter.

I shall be most grateful if you do not let my mother know that I have given you this information as I am sure it would upset her. She seems to be in a state of denial about her memory problems which, incidentally, are far worse than may have been apparent yesterday.

If Mother has to give up driving, I can take her to Sainsbury's once a week, and I expect that Social Services can recommend a local hairdresser who makes home visits. The only other regular car journeys she makes are to an exercise class, although I have gained the impression that she rarely goes there now. She can always use a taxi for that purpose.

Finally, I would appreciate it if I could be notified of the appointment with the specialist. Even if I am asked not to be present, it is important that I am made aware of his or her recommendations, as I am fairly confident that I will not learn of them from my mother.

Just over a week later, the GP wrote to Mother (with a copy to me) telling her that she should not drive and should inform the DVLA that she had received this advice. I rang Mother to discuss the letter. She thought it was unfair and did not accept that she was unfit to drive. I advised her of the potentially serious consequences of ignoring the letter, but she was unable to discuss the matter rationally. She rang me back later and I had to go through it with her all over again. We spoke at length the following day. She seemed both depressed and angry and was again incapable of rational discussion. Indeed, it was not until mid-April that she signed a letter to the DVLA, that I had drafted for her, notifying them that her doctor had advised her to stop driving. A short while later she was required to surrender her driving licence. I removed her car keys from her house.

The next day my mother rang me, having received a letter from an NHS psychiatrist to whom she had been referred by the GP. She was angry at the involvement of a psychiatrist and blamed me for it. She was very unpleasant and, when I got cross with her, she put the phone down on me.

The following day, 30th March, I drove to my mother's house to take her to the hairdresser and the supermarket. She wondered why I had got there so early. This puzzled me initially, but then I realised that she had not put her clocks forward an hour the previous weekend. She was, however, in a much better mood than yesterday, being far more positive. After the shopping was completed, I took her out for lunch. As I had had to hang around for about one and a half hours while she was having her hair done, it was agreed that, in future, we would arrange to have a hairdresser call at her home.

There was an incident around this time that indicated that my mother was not competent to handle even simple financial matters. She was late in paying her credit card statement for February, and the payment had not been received by Barclaycard by the time the March statement was issued. The only additional items on that statement were a late payment charge and an interest charge. She then paid that statement in full, having overlooked the fact that she had already paid the previous balance. I had to write a letter in her name in order to recover the over-payment. I was trying to deal with all her financial affairs, but she would sometimes forget my involvement, and problems like this could arise. It was very difficult to discuss these because she was highly sensitive to anything which she regarded as critical of her.

Another area of difficulty was her inability to remember the pin number for her debit card. She kept a written note of it in her handbag, which I told her not to do. To make matters worse, when asked at Sainsbury's to key in her pin number, she would sometimes take out her note and read the number aloud as she was keying it in. To stop this, I changed the number to her year of birth but even this failed to solve the problem.

The appointment with the psychiatrist was in early April. Anna and I were also present. Mother was surprisingly alert, although she failed two of the short-term memory tests. The psychiatrist diagnosed my mother with mild dementia. This surprised me. If her dementia was only regarded as mild, I wondered how bad it would have to be to be regarded as severe.

The following week I was due to take my mother to her exercise class and then on to the supermarket. I was not feeling well, and so Anna kindly took her instead. Anna told her on three separate occasions that I would be collecting her at 4:30 pm the next day to drive her over to our house. It had already been arranged that we would take her out for dinner, she would stay the night and, the following day, we would take her to see Eileen.

When I arrived at her house the next day, she had forgotten all of this. She was in bed, and I had to let myself in as she had not heard the doorbell. It took her until about 6:00 to get ready to leave. Things did not get any better. In the restaurant that evening she was not pleasant company: self-centred and grumpy. She was also unable to read the menu on the blackboard. She used to have very good eyesight for distance but, for some time, had worn glasses for reading. Latterly she had been prescribed varifocals but only seemed to wear them for watching television. I don't know whether this failure was the result of her dementia or her vanity. Possibly both.

The following afternoon we drove to Eileen's flat. Mother kept asking Eileen the same things, over and over again, and interrupting her with questions which had no relevance to what Eileen was saying. Eileen was shocked by the extent of her sister's deafness and vagueness. My mother was, in fact, wearing her NHS hearing aid but it was clearly ineffective. I suspect that either she did not know how to operate it, or the batteries had gone flat.

Two days later I had a frustrating telephone call from my mother who was hopelessly confused over the arrangements for her hairdresser to call at her home. We agreed, shortly thereafter, to abandon that idea and that, instead, I would take her to her village hairdresser once a week. By using that hairdresser, as opposed to the one four miles away, I would be able to go back to Mother's house while she was having her hair done, and deal with whatever jobs needed doing.

Because of my mother's difficulties in the restaurant, I rang her optician to arrange an eyesight test. I learned, however, from the telephone conversation that she had had a test six months earlier and had been diagnosed with cataracts in both eyes. She was supposed to have seen her GP about this but had not done so. I therefore made an appointment with the GP on her behalf. When I mentioned this to my mother, she had no recollection of having been informed she had cataracts.

When we saw the GP, she referred Mother to an eye specialist. I also took the opportunity to mention her increased deafness and obtained a referral to the audiology department of the nearest large hospital.

Anna and I were on holiday in France in early May when I received a call from a rather agitated Tom. He had discovered that Mother had an additional set of car keys, of which we had been unaware, and had been driving the car. I was inclined to think she was aware that she was no longer allowed to drive but did not appreciate the potential consequences of doing so. Tom appeared reluctant to confront her and he asked me what he should do. I told him to take the keys away with him when he went home.

On 18th May the new regime started whereby, on every Thursday morning, I would get to my mother's house about 9:30 to take her to the hairdresser, return to her house and then collect her when the hairdresser rang to say Mother was ready. From there I would drive her to Sainsbury's and walk round the supermarket with her to help with her shopping. Sometimes I would take her out to lunch and, on other occasions, we would have a light lunch at her house.

Two Thursdays later, I had a miserable day. I took Mother to a dentist's appointment at 9:00, followed by the hairdresser at 11:00. As usual she was not wearing a hearing aid and kept asking people to repeat themselves. We went back to her house for a light lunch where I had to shout to enable her to hear me. She then got ratty, saying that there was no need to shout. I, in turn, told her that I was fed up in having to repeat myself constantly and that she ought to wear her hearing aid. She maintained that I was the only person she had difficulty hearing, and that was because I mumbled. This caused me to blow my top and we had a row. In other circumstances I would have gone home but I could not that day as I had to take her to a hospital appointment with an eye specialist. Fortunately, by the time we got to the hospital, she had forgotten the row. The specialist confirmed the existence of the cataracts but as my mother was not aware of any deterioration in her sight and, in view of her age, surgery was not recommended at that stage.

Three weeks later, we had another bad day. As usual, I arrived at Mother's house at 9:30 to take her to the hairdresser for an appointment at 10:00. She greeted me in her dressing gown and was surprised to see me. I referred her to her diary, in which I had written my time of arrival and the hairdressing appointment. To my surprise both entries had been crossed through. When I asked her about this, she denied doing it and blamed my brother. I told her that that was ridiculous as he knew I was coming that day and there would have been no reason to make the deletions. I had to cancel the appointment. I had arranged a further appointment at 12:30, at her house, with a representative of the company from which my mother had bought her 'hidden' hearing aid. He gave her a hearing test for which she scored only 25%. She was advised that she ought to wear her aid every day and, indeed, ought to wear one in each ear. She promised me that she would wear it every day. There was, however, no realistic prospect of that promise being kept.

While I was with my mother that day she kept making derogatory remarks about her next-door neighbour. None of the matters complained of impinged on her in any way. She had simply developed a bee in her bonnet about the poor man.

One of the people who had kept in touch with Mother was a Chinese lady named Jenny who, many years ago, had been Tom's girlfriend. She had always been fond of my mother and, indeed, used to call her 'Mum.' One day in mid-July, I collected her from my local railway station and took her to see Mother. The latter was, unfortunately, in a depressed and confused state and the visit was not a success. Two days later I saw my mother again for the weekly hairdresser and supermarket visits, albeit a little later than usual. She was again very confused, informing me that two men had called to value the contents of her home and had left the valuation there. She did not know who they were or why they had called. I looked at the valuation and saw that it had been posted to her and was the result of a visit made by a single valuer, at the request of her contents insurers, about a month earlier, and when I was also present. She had forgotten that the second man was me.

The following week I drove Mother to hospital for an MRI scan on her brain which the psychiatrist had arranged. I took her out for lunch afterwards and then on to Sainsbury's.

On 25th July, I had a telephone call from a lady from the volunteer service in my mother's area. The volunteers use their own cars to provide transport to local elderly people. She had been given my number by the hairdresser (who had provided the voluntary service's details to Mother) and was seeking to clarify whether I would be taking my mother there on Thursday. It seems that Mother was confused and thought she was having her hair done that day (Tuesday) and needed a lift. To make matter worse, she kept forgetting she had made a call and ended up ringing both the voluntary service and the hairdresser about ten times each. I apologised to the woman who, fortunately, was very pleasant about it.

Two days later, on my weekly visit to Mother, I apologised to the hairdresser and took a box of chocolates with me. After returning from the supermarket, I mentioned to my mother the problems she had caused and that she had no need to trouble the voluntary service, as I acted as her driver. Moreover, I always put appointments in her diary so that she would know when I would be calling. She denied that she had made all the calls, accusing others of lying. We had an argument and I was so frustrated that I walked out. If my mother had accepted that she had a problem it would have been easier to handle, and I would have felt much more sympathetic towards her, but it was extremely rare for her to do so.

That incident reminds me of a story told to Anna by a friend. The friend's mother was also a widow suffering from dementia. She used to enjoy a couple of glasses of sherry before her evening meal. The problem was that she kept forgetting that she had already had her second glass, with the result that she was getting through bottles very quickly and spending most evenings somewhat inebriated.

In mid-August, Anna came with me on one of my weekly visits to my mother. We took her to the hairdresser and, from there, to Sainsbury's. We then went out to lunch but, on this occasion, Mother insisted on paying. She was not, however, on good form and kept repeating two topics which were then obsessing her. The first of these was that the key to the front of her grandfather clock, which had been converted to a drinks' cabinet, had been lost. She blamed this on Tom's son, Paul, who she said had visited her recently and had removed the key. She was angry about it. I had heard the accusation before and had spoken to Tom about it. Paul, at that time, was 13 years old and, although he had visited his grandmother with his father on one occasion that year, it was several months earlier. Tom and I both believed that the key had gone missing well after that visit. Although this was explained to Mother, she could not be persuaded. The other topic which obsessed her was a cheque that one of her gardeners had asked her to pay to his father. She did not know why this money had been paid. I had already investigated it and had seen from her chequebook stub that the sum in question was the same as she would normally have paid to her gardener. She had not been defrauded. It was simply that, for whatever reason, the gardener had wanted the money to go into his father's account. Again, my mother could not be persuaded that she had not been tricked into making the payment.

Later that afternoon, Mother had an appointment at her home with the psychiatrist. The scan had revealed that, owing to the furring-up of arteries, insufficient blood was getting through to the brain. The psychiatrist tested Mother's mental capacity again and this showed a deterioration since the previous test. She thought that my mother's condition was probably due to a combination of this lack of blood to the brain (vascular dementia), which may have been causing her to suffer mini-strokes, and Alzheimer's. She was showing symptoms of both. Mother gave no sign of understanding what was being said, probably because she could not hear. She was, however, quite aggressive and very repetitive during the consultation. When the psychiatrist commented that Mother was forgetful, the latter replied, "So would you be if you lived on your own." This was her usual response when anyone mentioned her memory, often said in an accusatory tone. The psychiatrist commented on the aggression and prescribed tablets to stabilise her memory.

On Wednesday of the following week, I received a call from my mother's hairdresser to tell me that Mother had rung both there and the voluntary service to change her appointment for the next day and to arrange a lift. I was asked if I could sort it out. I then rang Mother who was very confused. I confirmed that I would collect her in the morning at 9:45 and take her to have her hair done, as I had already written in her diary.

When I saw her the next day, she was in a better state, although still going on about Paul having lost her key.

Following the weekly visit at the end of August, I drove Mother to my house, and Anna and I took her out to dinner that evening. It was not an enjoyable occasion as Mother's memory span seemed to be no more than 30 seconds. Her main topic of conversation was her latest obsession: a desire to apply for a new driving licence.

The following morning Anna went out to buy some fish and meat which Mother had forgotten to get at the supermarket. Anna also brought back some forms for the driving licence application. We had a frank discussion with Mother about this and explained that she would have to disclose her confusion, forgetfulness and poor eyesight. These would prevent her from obtaining a licence. She simply refused to accept this. It was then left to me to complete the forms for her, which was a total waste of my time, and the application would also waste the time of her GP. Needless to say, the application failed. I recall, at about this time, testing her eyesight by asking her to read car number plates at a distance of about 20 metres. She could not do so but did not regard it as a reason for not being allowed to drive.

On my next weekly visit, Mother informed me that she had had a call from the DVLA to let her know that she could drive again. This 'call' was either an outright lie, a figment of her imagination or a telephone conversation that had taken place, in which she had misunderstood what had been said.

In early October, when collecting Mother from the hairdresser, the owner took me to one side and said that my mother had enquired as to the whereabouts of her pearl ring. Mother said she recalled the stone coming out of it and then giving the ring and the stone to a lady in the shop who said she would repair it. The salon owner was worried that I might think that either she, one of her staff, or a customer, had stolen it. I put the woman's mind at rest. When I got home I rang Tom and learned that the stone had become detached while Mother was staying with him; he had retained it so that he could have it repaired.

Towards the end of October there was another traumatic event that marked a further significant step in my mother's decline. I rang her at about 9:30 am on 24th October to remind her that I would be calling at 10:30. She sounded very miserable and said that she had slept badly and did not feel like going shopping. She said that Tom had been round the previous evening with two Japanese people and that, later, she had not been able to get into bed because she had found that the Japanese pair were in it. I told her she must have dreamt this, but I would come round and do the shopping for her on my own. When I arrived at her house, she looked dreadful; she had a black eye, a cut on her forehead, and a badly bruised right wrist and forearm. She was sitting in an armchair, in her dressing gown. She said that she had been coming down the stairs, carrying something, and had missed her footing, resulting in her falling down the last four steps. It appeared, moreover, that this accident had happened several days earlier, yet she had not telephoned anyone for help. I rang her GP's surgery and arranged for the GP to call round that afternoon and, in the meantime, I did the shopping and got her glasses repaired as a lens had fallen out in the accident. The GP referred Mother to the hospital for X-rays and an assessment. I told her that I would take my mother to my home for a few days and would call at the hospital on the way there.

We were at the hospital for about four hours. Mother had a thorough assessment. It was thought she had fractured her wrist; she had a urinary infection; and her neck was very painful as the muscles were in spasm. We did not get home until 11:00 pm. Mother spent most of the next day in bed. I had a call from a lady at the hospital who wanted Mother's details so that arrangements could be made for Social Services to carry out an assessment. That night Mother vomited in her bed, although we only found out about this in the morning. She was bilious again during the day and I called out a doctor from our practice. She advised that if my mother were no better the next day, she would refer her to hospital. In the event she was still unwell the following day and was taken to hospital by ambulance. I accompanied her, and remained with her for several hours, during which time she was seen by a consultant who arranged for her to have a brain scan.

My mother was in hospital for a month. During that time, either Anna or I, or both of us, visited her on most days. Tom drove down from London on a few occasions. Anna and I also called in, from time to time, at Mother's house to ensure that there were no problems, and to remove her post. On one such occasion, we went through the contents of her fridge/freezer and threw most of them out. The majority of items in the freezer section were several years old.

The reason my mother was in hospital for such a long time was not her physical injuries, but her mental condition. Various assessments she had had led to the conclusion that she was incapable of looking after herself. The hospital was not prepared to discharge her unless there was a suitable care package in place. This came as a relief to Tom and me as we had been trying to persuade Mother for months that she needed help, but she refused to accept that there was anything wrong with her.

In the days leading up to my mother's discharge from hospital I had a lot of jobs to do. These included considering various care packages and what she was able to afford; arranging for a locksmith to fit a key safe to the outside of her house so that carers could let themselves in, and also to change two of the locks to simplify them for her; helping Anna clean Mother's house; applying for Mother's Attendance Allowance (a State benefit then worth £48.50 a week, where frequent help was required during the day); arranging for the local pharmacy to provide her large variety of tablets in a dosset box (a means of organising the dispensing of tablets) so that the carers would know what medication to give her and when; interviewing a representative from the chosen care provider; installing batteries in the smoke alarms; photographing valuables in the house (in case of dishonesty on the part of a carer); and communicating with her GP.

Mother returned home on 28th November. Tom and I persuaded her, for security purposes, to let us take care of her chequebook and the key to her safe. Two days later, Anna and I went to see her so that we could be present when she had a further assessment by the psychiatrist. Whilst there, we met the principal carer from the agency we had chosen, a pleasant lady named Pamela. She or a colleague would call in three times a day to get Mother's meals and ensure she took her medication. A cleaner from the agency also called once a week. After a short while, Pamela was persuaded to include the cleaning as part of her duties, as Mother liked her.

In preparation for the meeting with the psychiatrist, I wrote her a letter which I handed to her as she arrived, and which she was able to read before the assessment.

I will be giving you this note tomorrow in case I am unable to speak freely in front of my mother.

My brother, my wife and I are all of the opinion that Mother is no longer in a position to manage her affairs. She appears to be incapable of absorbing information, forgetting what she has been told within seconds. Although I look after her financial affairs, she retains her debit card and is entitled to a chequebook (although I removed her current chequebook yesterday).

The following examples illustrate the reasons for our concerns:

Mother has great difficulty in remembering her pin number, even though it is her year of birth. Even when she can remember, she tends to say it aloud.

When I make a payment on her behalf, she cannot remember that she has repaid me and keeps asking me to tell her how much she owes.

Several months ago, she paid a cheque in somewhat strange circumstances and has become obsessed that she has been defrauded. It was, fortunately, not for a significant amount. When asked why she wrote the cheque, her only explanation is that she had been asked to do so.

She is easy prey to 'cold callers,' as is apparent from the number of times she has changed her utility suppliers, which causes me a lot of aggravation, especially as she cannot remember having made the change.

You may recall that my brother and I hold an Enduring Power of Attorney. As we believe that our mother has become, or is becoming, mentally incapable, we are under a duty to apply to the Court of Protection to register the EPA. This gives rise to a potentially serious problem. As you are probably aware, before making the Court application, the Attorney(s) must give notice of the proposed registration to the Donor (i.e. Mother) and to at least three relatives. Although my brother and I count as two of those relatives, it will be necessary for us to give notice to the next class of relatives, i.e. her sisters. The law requires that if one member of a class is notified, then all people in that class must be notified. It will be clear to our mother from the notice that my brother and I consider she is no longer mentally capable. Moreover, if she reads the notice carefully, she will realise that other people are being notified of that. This is likely to cause her a great deal of distress, especially if she were to learn that her three sisters have been notified. As you have probably realised, my mother retains a high opinion of herself and is ultra-sensitive. As a consequence, we all have to be very careful in the way we handle her. Although she is very forgetful, she tends to remember things that have upset her.

The law does allow exemptions from the requirement to give notice in exceptional circumstances. Dispensation, however, will normally only be given where it can be shown that the Donor would be unduly harmed or distressed by the news. I shall be grateful if you will consider this aspect of the matter and, if you consider it appropriate, let me have a letter, which can accompany the Court application, in support of my request for dispensation.

If, of course, you are strongly of the opinion that my mother is mentally capable, we will reconsider our proposed course of action.

The assessment revealed that Mother's mental state had deteriorated significantly, and the doctor had no hesitation in advising her that I should now take over her financial affairs under a power of attorney. (It was in fact a power of attorney under which Tom and I were to act jointly.) She was not, however, prepared to commit herself to supporting the proposed application for dispensing with the need to serve my mother with formal notice. In the circumstances Tom and I decided not to apply for dispensation.

The power of attorney had been signed in July 2004 and I now gave notice to my mother and her sisters of my intention to register it with the Court of Protection. As far as my mother was concerned, I handed her the notice on one of my weekly visits, together with various other papers. She did not comment on it, and I am sure that either she did not read it properly or, if she did, she did not properly understand it.

My mother had been a difficult woman for many years but, as her dementia increased, I found it highly stressful to be in her company for any length of time. Unfortunately, her state of health meant that I had to see a great deal of her. With her discharge from hospital I would have to resume visiting her at home and spending more time with her. This affected my health, and at the beginning of December I saw my GP who prescribed an antidepressant and referred me to a counsellor/psychotherapist. More on this later. Now that carers were in place, there was no longer any need to take my mother shopping every week. Anna would do the shopping for her at the same time as she did our own. As the carers were preparing her food, we provided a variety of frozen meals each week for them to heat up, plus fresh vegetables and fruit. If anything for the house was needed, the carers would let us know.

I still went to see my mother every week to deliver the groceries and to deal with any post or other matters. This included calling at the pharmacy to collect the dosset box containing the tablets for the forthcoming week. During the second week of December I went to see her twice. On the first occasion, as well as taking the groceries, I brought with me a batch of Christmas cards. I had had to work out to whom she sent cards, and to address the envelopes. All she had to do was sign them. This was just as well as she did not remember several of the recipients. That was not the only problem. I had learned from one of her sisters that, the previous year, she had received three separate cards from Mother.

On the same visit I stuck a notice on the front door reminding my mother not to touch the knob on the lock or leave the keys in the bottom lock. Doing one of those things would prevent the carer from gaining access with the key from the key safe, which had happened on one or more occasions. On the second visit that week, Anna came with me so that she could find out how many of Mother's clothes still fitted, as she had put on a lot of weight in recent months. The answer was, not many. We also told her that we would be buying her two pairs of shoes for Christmas and asked her to choose these from a selection I had printed from the Internet. These were 'sensible' shoes which were designed for comfort and mobility, rather than the narrow shoes, with very high heels, that she habitually wore. She was no longer steady on her feet and we suspected that her shoes may have been responsible for her fall down the stairs in October. Furthermore, there was something rather ludicrous about a woman of 82 tottering around in very high heels. To my relief, she chose a couple of pairs. On earlier occasions the subject had been raised, she had refused to accept that she needed to wear a different type of shoe.

On Christmas Eve, Anna and I collected Mother and brought her to our home for Christmas, as usual. Anna helped her to pack her bag. Later that day, Sarah made her annual observation of how much worse her grandmother's memory and confusion had become.

On Christmas Day, I drove to Eileen's and brought her home. She and Maggie talked to each other almost non-stop for the rest of the day. During the opening of the Christmas presents, Mother's lack of enthusiasm for her new shoes was quite apparent. I reminded her that she had chosen them herself, but she had no recollection of that. I later heard her complaining to Eileen about them, saying that she would never have chosen them. I later removed them, and they were returned to the supplier.

We took Mother home after lunch on 27th December.

Chapter Ten

2007

Andrew and Morag were with us for a few days over the New Year. On New Year's Day they went to see Mother. I called to see her the following day to take her to the hairdresser. While there, she asked me whether I had her chequebook and I confirmed that I did. She said she wanted it back. I reminded her that Tom and I were looking after her financial affairs and that she did not need to write any cheques. She insisted that I should hand it back and became unpleasant when I said I could not do that. This type of situation, of which this was merely an example, was difficult to handle as, to spare her feelings, I could not simply tell the truth which was that she lacked the mental capacity to deal with her financial affairs.

In early January, I took Mother's car to her local garage for its MOT certificate. Tom had indicated that he might buy it for his eldest daughter or, if she did not want it, he would try to sell it. So, a few days later, I collected Tom from my local station and drove him to Mother's. He was going to drive her to London in her car and she would stay with him for a few days.

Even though she had been told of the arrangements, and they were in her diary, she was not even dressed when we arrived at about 12:15. She was in a cantankerous mood, complaining that the skirts that Anna had had let out for her were too big in the waist. Admittedly, she had a point. She also referred to the carers. She wanted to know whose idea it was that she should have them, and how much they cost. She did not want them to come any more. When informed of the cost, she was horrified. We explained that the Social Services had not been prepared to allow her to return to her home unless carers were employed. We put it to her gently that she was no longer able to look after herself properly. She responded that the carers were not doing anything for her. When we pointed that they were getting her meals, and were also cleaning the house, she maintained that she was doing these things for herself. That, of course, was nonsense. I knew exactly what the carers were doing as they had to maintain a register setting out the time of arrival and departure of each visit, what they had done each time, including details of the food provided, and my mother's mood or state of health. I cannot now remember if this was the first time my mother had raised the subject of the carers, but it was certainly not the last. It became another obsession. Tom and I ended up having an argument with her. Tom also had the pleasure of driving her to London and putting her up (and putting up with her) for the next few days.

The register that the carers maintained also contained general information on my mother's condition and mentioned Alzheimer's. I instructed the carers to ensure that the register was kept on the top shelf of one of the kitchen cupboards so that Mother could not see it. One day a carer failed to do this. Mother looked through the register and saw the reference to Alzheimer's. This enraged her. When Pamela next came round,

99

my mother tore into her, vehemently denying that she had Alzheimer's and blaming Pamela for telling lies. Poor Pamela had had nothing to do with it.

Even though my mother was away for a few days, staying with Tom, she still occupied part of my time. I managed to catch up with her paperwork; I met with a plumber at her house who investigated some problems in her central heating system; and I produced a schedule of her income and expenses in preparation for a meeting with my financial adviser, who was now also advising on her investments. Although she usually thanked me for taking her to the hairdresser, she had little or no idea of the amount of work I did for her behind the scenes. This added to a sense of grievance on my part. Instead of gratitude, I had to suffer frequent nastiness.

This is probably a good time to return to the counselling I was having at that time. I started in early December, and had about a dozen sessions, spread over a few months. My mother was driving me to distraction, and I found it helpful to be able to talk openly to a perceptive and sympathetic third party. However, whilst I felt better during and after each session, I do not think that, ultimately, the course was of enduring benefit. In fact, my wife thought it had the reverse effect, and she was probably right. As well as being stressed, I was frustrated at having to suffer a great deal of unpleasantness from my mother, yet not being able to do anything about it. This was because, as a matter of filial duty, I had had to assume responsibility for all aspects of her life (Tom did comparatively little as he did not live near her) and, in any event, because of her mental state, giving her a piece of my mind was unlikely to have had any lasting effect. Presumably with this in mind, the counsellor asked me to write a letter to my mother, which would never be sent, in which I let her know what I thought of her. It was, I think, intended to be an outpouring of my feelings which would prove therapeutic. Unfortunately, the document I produced was probably too analytical and too thorough. By the time I completed it, my dislike of my mother was more intense than ever. I should make it clear, however, that I am not being critical of counselling. It can be of benefit to many people. It just did not, ultimately, work for me.

The power of attorney was registered with the Court of Protection in early 2007, but not much else of consequence took place at that time. Mother was often miserable, which was hardly surprising. There were several times she was not ready when I arrived to take her to her appointment with the hairdresser. I kept reminding her to check her diary, but she simply could not remember to do so. I recall getting cross with her on one of these occasions when she revealed her innate selfishness. After pointing out to her that we would be very late, she replied to the effect: "Let them wait. It won't hurt them." I also had to cancel the appointment twice within three weeks as Mother said she was not feeling well. There did not seem to be anything wrong with her (apart from the obvious, which she would not acknowledge), and I think it was a case of her not wanting to make the effort to go.

It was also at that time that my mother developed another of her obsessions. At some stage she became aware that she had lost her watch and became convinced that it had happened at our house, just before she went into hospital. She said that the last time she had seen it was when it was on the dressing table in the guest room in which she was sleeping. I suggested that it may have gone missing when she was in hospital, but she was adamant that she did not have it there. She came very close to saying that one of my family had stolen it. The following week, at the end of February, I drove over to my mother's house to take her to hospital for an appointment with the audiology department. My diary records that, on the 30-minute drive to the hospital, we had a major row, although it does not mention the subject. I think, however, that this may have been the first occasion that she accused my daughter of stealing the watch: an accusation that was to be repeated often, and for which there was no justification whatsoever. Even if Sarah were the type of person who would have stolen her grandmother's watch, which she most certainly is not, she could not have done so as she was not even in the house at the time of the alleged theft, having moved to London a few years earlier. It is possibly germane to mention at this stage that the timepiece in question was of little value.

At the hospital my mother was given a pair of digital hearing aids and an explanation of how to use them. It was clear to me, driving home from the hospital, that she was not going to wear them much, if at all. She complained that they were too big, even though they would have been hidden by her hair. It was also apparent that she had not understood the simple process of how to operate them.

I visited my mother again the next day, which was one of the occasions that her trip to the hairdresser was cancelled, and I found her sitting in her dressing gown reading the newspaper. She was not wearing the hearing aids and said she did not need to do so as she was on her own. I then found that she had not disconnected them after taking them off the previous evening, so that the batteries had been running all night. I wrote her a note explaining what she had to do with the devices and told her that it would be for her own benefit, and that of other people, if she could hear what was said to her. I explained that it was very frustrating for people to have to repeat themselves frequently. She then told me that she did not want me coming to see her as there was always 'aggro.' Unfortunately, I was not in a position to comply with her request.

In the first week of March, I rang my mother to tell her that I had made an appointment with the hairdresser for the following day. I asked her to write it in her diary, but she declined to do so on the basis that she would not forget. Her inability to recognise her own shortcomings was extraordinary.

That evening she telephoned me and was aggressive, accusing me of removing the key to her safe without her agreement. She had, of course, forgotten that she had given me the key so that nobody else would be able to access the safe, which contained some valuable pieces of jewellery. She went on to say that she did not trust me.

The following morning, I had an appointment with the counsellor. After leaving her, I telephoned my mother to remind her of the hairdressing appointment. She had forgotten about it. When I arrived at her house 25 minutes later, at 11:45, she was still not washed or dressed. Fortunately, she managed to be ready in time. I had lunch with her later. The carer had left her something to eat and I bought my lunch at the sandwich shop/deli near the hairdresser. We spoke very little over our meal.

At about 7:15 pm the next day I received a telephone call from one of the carers who reported that Mother was in bed and did not want anything to eat. She said that Mother had been acting in a more demented manner recently, and kept on about her watch, saying that my daughter had stolen it. I explained that this was nonsense, and the carer said she realised that that was the case. It is not unusual for dementia sufferers to make false accusations.

Although Tom and I had removed our mother's chequebook after she was discharged from hospital, now that the power of attorney was in force she was not, in any event, entitled to write cheques. She paid the hairdresser and her gardeners in cash and I ensured each week that she had sufficient in her purse. When I called to see her in the second week of March, I gave her £50 in cash which, on this occasion, caused her to become resentful over her lack of a chequebook. I patiently tried to explain the reason for this, but she would not accept it.

To give me a break, Anna went to see my mother the following week and took the opportunity to explain that it was very wrong of her to tell people that Sarah had stolen her watch. Mother categorically denied ever doing so.

The flowers I had ordered for Mothering Sunday had apparently not been delivered (in fact, they had; she had forgotten having received them) and so, on my next visit to my mother, I took a bouquet. She was very pleased with this and was in a good mood for a change. On returning from the hairdressers, we had a sandwich lunch together. After that I took her jewellery out of the safe and she enjoyed looking at it for a while. She was also fine when she came to stay with us over the Easter weekend (when Andrew and Morag were also present) and, indeed, there were no further untoward incidents until early May.

On 8th May, I again took Jenny (Tom's girlfriend of many years ago) to see my mother. After the latter's trip to the hairdresser, I took the two of them out for a pub lunch. Later, when I was in Mother's kitchen, putting away the shopping I brought earlier, I could hear Mother talking to Jenny in the sitting room. Mother was, as usual, speaking loudly. She was telling her about Sarah stealing the watch. I wished to avoid a scene and said nothing at the time. I did, however, explain to Jenny, when driving her back to the station, that the story was untrue. When I got home, I telephoned Mother to tell her to stop spreading this nonsense. She denied saying anything of the sort to Jenny. She accused her of being a troublemaker by making up the story. I made it clear that Jenny was not the source, and that I had overheard the conversation. Even then she maintained the denial. The conversation became heated, and I ended it abruptly. Later that evening, she rang me and there was a repetition of the earlier conversation. She clearly did not appreciate the absurdity of attributing to Jenny something of which Jenny would have had no knowledge if she had not been informed of it by Mother. This was one of those occasions when she was impossible to deal with.

Two days later Jenny telephoned me to say that Mother had rung accusing her of causing trouble by lying to me over what had been said. Later Tom and I spoke over the phone. He had been to see Mother that day and she had been ranting about Jenny. He seemed to be blaming me for raising the issue with Mother. I wonder whether, if he knew that his mother was telling everyone she met that one of his children was a thief, he would have challenged her. Anyway, we both felt sorry that Jenny had been treated so badly, and I sent her some flowers with an apologetic message.

The next day Jenny contacted me, and I reported on this in an email to my brother.

Jenny rang me this morning to thank me for the flowers and to say that the only apology that was due was from Mum, but she realised that Mum was mentally ill. She said that if she had been a troublemaker, she would have repeated stories for years as Mum was always talking about other people. This accords with a remark that Pamela made to me on Tuesday. She indicated that she was having difficulty in getting the cleaning done as Mother was talking to her all the time. She then added something to the effect that there is nothing she doesn't know about the family!

Later that day Jenny called me again to report that my mother had rung her twice that day and left messages. She was demanding that Jenny should apologise to Anna and me for telling lies about Sarah. She made an unspecified threat as to the consequences if Jenny failed to do so. Jenny asked me to erase her details from my mother's address book, which I did.

Andrew and Morag were getting married in early July and Tom's eldest daughter, Jo, was due to be married in late July. Mother frequently mentioned the latter whilst forgetting about Andrew's wedding. She subsequently decided not to go to his wedding on the basis that it was taking place in Edinburgh, which was a long way to go at her age. If she had gone, it would have been with Tom and his family, so she would have been looked after. I am possibly being unreasonable, but I cannot help thinking that a loving grandmother would have made the effort and wondering whether she would have gone if it had been Tom's daughter who was marrying there. (Jo's wedding was in fact called off at a late stage.)

The following week, when driving to my mother's, I got held up in traffic. Concerned that this would impact on her hairdressing appointment, I called her on my mobile to explain that I would be late and asked her to be ready to leave as soon as I arrived. She was not, and we were late. Subsequently, she started on again about Jenny having always been a troublemaker and that she (Mother) had not said anything to her about Sarah. There was no point in arguing with her. I find it interesting that she appeared to have no recollection of what had actually occurred but a wholly false version had become firmly embedded in her brain.

Anna kindly made two of the next three weekly visits to my mother, and after that we were away for three weeks. Tom filled in with the shopping and hairdresser duties. When I returned he was suitably stressed.

I next saw my mother twice at the beginning of July. On the second occasion, she had an appointment with a colleague of her psychiatrist. She had initially been prescribed Galantamine, a medication to assist with the dementia, but it seemed this was giving her diarrhoea. As a result of the consultation, she was prescribed Aricept, a similar medication.

Anna and I were then away in Scotland for a week's holiday, which took in Andrew and Morag's wedding. Mother was suffering with her stomach when I saw her on my return. On visiting her the following week, I was treated to another rant over Jenny having lied to me. She refused to accept that Jenny had not done so, and that I had overheard the conversation. This had become her latest obsession but, at least, she was no longer complaining about Sarah.

At the end of July, I rang my mother at 9:15 to say that Anna and I would take her to lunch after her hairdressing appointment that day, so she should tell her carer not to make her a sandwich. She then mentioned that she could not find her bank card, and I reminded her that I had taken it away as there was a power of attorney in operation. This caused her to become agitated, indicating that she knew little or nothing about the power of attorney. She told me she did not want to be taken out to lunch and put the phone down on me. When Anna and I arrived at her house, she was still in her dressing gown and had clearly forgotten about her appointment. She had to ring the hairdresser to cancel it. She told us she did not feel well. We concluded that she felt miserable but had forgotten why. She appeared not to remember being angry over the telephone. We again offered to take her to lunch but she declined. By the time we left, her mood had improved.

The local pharmacy was delivering the dosset box each week, which saved me the task of collecting it. However, I had to do so on my visit to Mother in the first week of August as she had failed to hear the doorbell when the delivery man called. Her unwillingness to wear her hearing aids was a frequent cause of difficulties. Indeed, I believe that it may have been a contributory factor in her dementia in that it increased her isolation. It is no fun trying to converse with someone when you have to keep repeating yourself, and almost shout to be heard. The dementia made the situation even worse because she kept repeating herself as she could not remember what had been said only a few seconds earlier. I used to dread my weekly visits.

*

Andrew and Morag came to stay with us over the bank holiday at the end of August and I took them to see Eileen. Although she was showing signs of dementia, and twittered away constantly, her mental state was far better than my mother's. Moreover, Eileen had very good hearing. She also always seemed pleased to see me.

*

My weekly visits to my mother continued without major incident for several weeks. On one such occasion we chatted about Andrew and it was apparent that she had forgotten he was now married and had no idea what he did for a living. She was also suffering again from diarrhoea and, some time later, after having blood tests, was taken off the Aricept tablets which had been prescribed for her dementia.

It may have been about this time, after staying with Tom for a few days, that she developed a dislike of one of his daughters. She would reiterate this dislike quite often, even though she could possibly no longer remember the reason for it.

At the end of October, I arrived at my mother's at 11:30 to take her to the hairdresser. She was not washed or dressed, having forgotten her appointment which I had to cancel. She was due to see her GP that afternoon and I ended up staying with her for about four and a half hours. It was a severe endurance test. She appeared to be suffering from depression and complained of feeling ill. She denied that, however, when the doctor came. Perhaps she had forgotten.

In mid-November I had another long session with Mother. I took her for a hospital appointment and we then went out for lunch. She was in a good mood, insisting that I should reimburse myself out of her account. She had, by this time, got used to the idea that I was dealing with her finances. On the way back to her house, I did her food shopping. In all I spent almost six hours with her, returning home exhausted.

On a visit in early December, Mother was very slow in getting ready to go out and got irritable when I tried to hurry her up. In the end she was ten minutes late for the hairdresser, but her attitude was simply, "Too bad!" On the same visit I took her Christmas cards for signature, for which I had again prepared addressed envelopes.

On the following visit, her mental state seemed to have deteriorated. This may have been caused by her coming off Aricept. She appeared unable to retain anything I said to her and I came home feeling miserable. To give me a break, Anna made the next weekly trip. When checking to see how much cash Mother had in her purse, Anna found it was £20 less than it should have been. She asked Mother whether she had given her gardeners cash for Christmas but was told she had not as she always gave them a bottle of wine each (which Anna had taken with her). I later rang one of the gardeners who told me that my mother had given him and his colleague £10 each for Christmas the previous week. As I have mentioned before, the only cash payments she had to make were to the gardeners and the hairdresser. This was not the only occasion she had been unable to explain a cash shortfall.

Andrew and Morag stayed with us over Christmas. Eileen came for Christmas Day, and Mother was with us for three days. After I had sent Eileen home in a taxi on the evening of Christmas Day, Mother commented on how tired she felt. I said that I was not surprised as she and Eileen had been talking all day without a break. She denied she had been talking a lot, claiming it was Eileen.

Mother's short-term memory seemed to be no more than a few seconds, which did not enhance our Christmas. Fortunately, Andrew and Morag were remarkably patient with her. On 28th December, I telephoned her to let her know that she had left her watch here. This was a replacement for the one she believed Sarah had stolen. She was under the impression that we had stayed at Anna's family home over Christmas, not realising that she had been at our house.

CHAPTER ELEVEN

2008

THERE WAS ANOTHER EXAMPLE IN JANUARY OF MY mother not hearing the pharmacy's delivery man ringing the doorbell, so that I had to drive to the pharmacy to collect the dosset box. It was just as well I had had a key safe fitted to the outside of her house, as otherwise there would have been many occasions when the carers would not have been able to get in. There was not just a problem with her hearing, but also with her mobility. At some stage, although I am now not certain when it occurred, she began to use a walking stick. So, even if she heard the doorbell, it was quite likely that the driver would have gone by the time she opened the door. If she did not have her stick available, she would move around indoors by supporting herself on pieces of furniture as she walked past them. She was still wearing high heels.

Anna and I went to Mother's house later in January to take her out to lunch for her birthday. First, we gave her a watch that Tom and I had bought as her birthday present. She liked it, although within a matter of hours, and probably less, she would have forgotten who gave it to her or even that it was new. The subsequent lunch turned out to be amusing. The restaurant we had chosen was situated by a river. When we arrived, it was apparent that the river had burst its banks in places. Fortunately, the car park and access to the building were not affected. However, while we were eating our desserts, a waitress came round to the occupied tables to announce that there had been a flood warning and that we were advised to leave promptly after finishing our meals. Mother did not hear what the waitress had said and showed no sign of hurrying. Anna and I had finished eating but Mother just carried on talking. Other diners were leaving but she was oblivious to the exodus. We were becoming anxious. I explained the problem to her and that we needed to leave. She made it clear that she did not believe me and that I was just making an excuse to go. By the time we managed to do so, the water had covered much of the car park and obscured the driveway to the road. Driving away was a scary experience yet, when I mentioned the incident to Mother a day or so later, she had no recollection of it.

*

I had spoken to Eileen the previous week and she was in a confused state. Before going to Mother's, I rang Eileen to find out how she was. She was still confused and felt too dizzy to go shopping. I therefore asked her to make a list of her requirements, so that I could do the shopping for her the following day. When calling on her with it, I went in to see the warden of the sheltered accommodation to ensure that she was aware of Eileen's problems. She was. Eileen was not slow in letting the warden know of her various ailments.

Sheltered accommodation does not suit everybody, but it was ideal for Eileen. Following Bob's death, almost nine years earlier, she had become rather solitary. She had been finding it difficult to cope with living on her own in a bungalow and welcomed being released from some of the administrative burdens it involved. She was also lucky to have a lady, named Beryl, in the flat opposite, who was far more socially active. They would go shopping together and Beryl encouraged Eileen to join her at the residents' morning coffee session. The residents, who were mainly elderly ladies, had other social activities, such as bingo once or twice a week, although Eileen did not attend those often. The warden was available during weekday mornings.

Being in a community was also beneficial for Eileen as she was impractical in many ways. An example of this occurred in relation to a shredder that I bought her for Christmas one year, after she had mentioned that she would like one. She telephoned me shortly after Christmas to say that the plug did not fit her sockets. I could not understand this as I recalled it was a standard three-pin plug. I therefore drove over to Eileen's to try to solve the problem, only to discover that she had simply failed to remove the plastic cover from the three pins.

*

My mother used to be unkind, behind Eileen's back, about various aspects of Eileen's accommodation and lifestyle, especially the communal bingo. She got it into her head that Eileen was playing every night of the week and, despite numerous efforts on my part to disabuse her of this, it remained lodged there.

The day after visiting Eileen with the shopping, I was back at my mother's to be present for an appointment with one of the Health Authority's psychiatrists. After testing her, he informed me that her memory and orientation had deteriorated since she was tested a year earlier. He advised that her dementia could be categorised as mild/moderate. He said he would arrange for her to be tested to see if she was suitable to go to a day centre.

*

The following day I had a long telephone conversation with a community psychiatrist who had seen Eileen earlier in the week. She told me that Eileen was to be assessed the following week. It was, however, apparent that she needed some assistance from Social Services for which she had said she was willing to pay.

*

There were no further untoward incidents with my mother until the end of February when a dispute arose with the care agency. I received a telephone call from Pamela one evening. She explained that she had a problem with her back, because of which she did not feel able to carry on doing the cleaning for my mother. She would, however, continue as a carer. This annoyed my mother who, in a fit of pique, rang the agency to tell them that she did not want Pamela to come any more. The agency removed Pamela from the contract. Pamela telephoned me to explain why she would no longer be going to my mother's house. I was dismayed by this turn of events. Tom and I liked Pamela as, indeed, had my mother hitherto.

The following morning, I rang the agency and explained that Tom and I were their client, and not our mother, and that they were not entitled to remove Pamela from the care contract without first consulting us. I said I wanted her reinstated. The employee I spoke to said she would refer the matter to the manager. The same day Tom went to see Mother on his weekly visit. He was unable to persuade her to change her mind. It was clear from his visit, and from a telephone conversation I had with her, that she did not understand that Pamela's role as cleaner was in addition to her duties as a carer. She maintained that Pamela was only a cleaner and did not perform any other functions. Mother continued to believe that she got her own meals and dealt with her own medication. She was angry with Pamela and appeared to regard Pamela's conduct as an act of betrayal.

There were further telephone conversations the next day on this vexed issue. The new manager at the care agency apologised for being unaware of the power of attorney. She maintained, however, that "your mother had been very distressed" over Pamela and that, as the agency owed Mother a duty of care, it was inappropriate for Pamela to continue. I explained that my mother was not 'distressed' but 'obsessed' by Pamela not being prepared to do the cleaning any more, and that she did not understand the duties of a carer. I nevertheless appreciated the difficult position in which the agency had been placed and, on being assured that Pamela would not be prejudiced by the matter, I decided not to pursue it further. I spoke to Pamela to report on my conversation and apologised for my mother's behaviour. She acknowledged that my mother's illness was the cause of her behaviour. She told me that she was unhappy with the agency in any event and would be leaving to join another one. I offered to provide her with a reference if she needed one.

I saw my mother a few days later and there was a difficult discussion in relation to Pamela. Mother was unable to follow the simplest of arguments. She failed to show the slightest remorse for any harm that she had caused.

It would possibly have been about this time that I took either a watch or a clock belonging to my mother to be repaired. When returning it to her, I informed her of the cost. Instead of thanking me, she remarked, "They must have seen you coming." This expression, which she had picked up from my father, indicated that the repairer had seen that I was a mug and had overcharged me. There was not only a lack of gratitude, but also gratuitous rudeness.

Having been unimpressed with the care agency over the way they had handled the problem with Pamela, I decided to replace them. When my mother was next at the hairdresser, I had a meeting with two representatives of the company that Pamela was joining. It went well, and they were appointed with effect from the beginning of April. In the meantime, I was present at my mother's house when she was interviewed by a lady from Social Services to assess Mother's suitability for a day centre. It was fortunate that I was present as Mother was painting a very false picture of her activities and capabilities. She again asserted that she did all her own cooking and general housework.

The new care company started on 1st April. That coincided with my weekly visit. They did not get off to the best of starts as the carer had omitted to make Mother's lunch. I made it instead. On my visit the following week my mother was pleasant and appreciative. This was so unusual that I made a diary note of it.

When I went to see her in the third week of April, with the shopping, she was still in her dressing gown, having forgotten her hairdressing appointment, which I cancelled. She was complaining about a painful hip which, she said, had kept her awake during the night. The following week, when I went, she was in bed, feeling ill. I again had to cancel her visit to the hairdresser. I felt sorry about all these late cancellations, but there was nothing I could do about it. I also cancelled Mother's visit to the day centre which had been due to take place the following day. She did not seem to me to be physically ill, but I nevertheless arranged for her GP to call round later in the day.

Sarah was due to get married to her boyfriend, Jonathan, in July, with the reception being held in a marquee in our garden. Anna did the weekly trip to Mother's at the beginning of June so that she could check which, if any, of Mother's outfits still fitted. It was a somewhat fraught experience as Mother was uncooperative and indicated that she did not wish to accept the wedding invitation. While I was rather hurt by this, I was not unduly surprised and, to be honest, quite relieved. We decided not to attempt to persuade her to change her mind.

When I arrived at my mother's the following week at 11:30, she was still in her dressing gown and I had the impression that she had only just got up. Again, she complained of feeling ill, although there did not seem to be much wrong with her apart from a painful hip. I asked my mother whether the carer had reminded her that I was coming. She said that she had not seen the carer. I read the carers' attendance register and saw that the reminder had been recorded. So, not only had Mother forgotten the appointment, she had forgotten being reminded about it, and could not even recall seeing the carer who had also made her breakfast. Mother was in a bad mood and was constantly repeating herself. I felt depressed for the rest of the day. There was, however, one small mercy. The agency was using Pamela as Mother's principal carer and either Mother had forgotten that she had been angry with Pamela, or she had forgiven Pamela now that the latter, her back having recovered, was prepared to carry on with the cleaning.

Two days later, I had a telephone message from Pamela that water was leaking into my mother's bathroom. I had been working in the garden, doing some preparatory work for Sarah's wedding. I had to stop what I was doing, contact HomeServe, with whom my mother had an emergency plumbing insurance policy, and arrange to meet a plumber at Mother's house. The plumber solved the problem and I drove home. I received no thanks from my mother.

Mother was being difficult generally at that time and I have diary notes of telephone conversations with the care agency and with the day centre. The psychiatrist who had last seen my mother had felt that it would be beneficial for her to go to the day centre a couple of times a week, as she would be able to socialise with other people of a similar age. She would be there for several hours and would be given lunch. Unfortunately, it meant her getting up a little earlier than usual and she could not be bothered to make the effort.

I also have diary notes at that time of the difficulties I was having in dealing with my mother's cash investments in banks and building societies. Some of these institutions appeared not to know how to handle powers of attorney, and caused me a good deal of frustration.

When I saw Mother in the second week of July, she appeared to have forgotten that Sarah was due to get married later that month and was not particularly interested to learn that Morag was pregnant. I made a diary note, on my visit the following week, that she was cheerful. That was quite a rare occurrence at that time.

I saw my mother at the end of July, a few days after the wedding, when she had an appointment with her psychiatrist. She was hateful that day. First, she showed no interest in Sarah's wedding when I tried to tell her about it. A little later, when the psychiatrist asked why she had not gone to the wedding, she told her that she had not been invited. I made it clear that she had declined to attend. After the psychiatrist left I had to take Mother to the hairdresser. When we returned, I told her that it was wrong of her to say she had not been asked to the wedding. This increased her bad mood. Shortly afterwards she received a visit from the assistant to the community psychiatric nurse. I was not in the room for the whole of this visit, but I heard her repeatedly praising Tom's children to this woman, whilst barely mentioning Sarah or Andrew. She also made a derogatory remark about me, which I did not hear properly. I believe that lauding Tom and his family whilst denigrating me was her way of getting back at me for having told her off.

When I next saw her, I let her know how much her behaviour had upset me the previous week. She could not, of course, remember it and could not even recall the CPN's assistant coming. There was no apology forthcoming and she became defensive. Strong words were exchanged but, by the time I collected her from the hairdresser, she had forgotten all about it and was in a good mood.

I understood that my mother's dementia was responsible for her confusion and loss of memory. I was also aware that the illness can result in personality changes, although that has not been apparent with other dementia sufferers I know. In my mother's case, those changes seemed to be accentuations of pre-existing flaws in her personality and it was mainly this that made her behaviour so hard to accept. Indeed, it could be said that her true personality became manifest as she was less inhibited in what she said. (Dementia can affect a person's inhibitions, making them more likely to say or do things they ordinarily would not.) She was a difficult woman before she became ill; afterwards, she became insufferable at times. I had an interesting conversation with one of my neighbours a few years ago. He runs two or three care homes and so has experience of

119

the various types of dementia. His own mother suffered from vascular dementia and, without any prompting from me, it was clear that he held very similar views about her to those I have just expressed about my mother. Those views are also supported by anecdotal evidence from family carers posting on the members' forums of websites such as those operated by the Alzheimer's Society and AgingCare.

Occasionally, my mother's confusion could produce some grimly amusing moments. For example, when I saw her in mid-July, she informed me that Tom had just married Ruth. They had, by that time, been married for about 32 years.

*

To make matters worse, Eileen's mental state appeared to deteriorate significantly. In mid-August I telephoned her to say that we would not be able to have her for Christmas that year. I explained that Andrew and Morag were expecting a baby on Christmas Eve and that Morag was booked into their local hospital. In the circumstances they would be unable to spend Christmas at our house and Andrew had suggested that we stay with them. We had accepted the invitation as we wanted to be in a position to be of help to them, especially as Morag's parents live in Scotland. Andrew and Morag would be unable to put up my mother and so she would be spending Christmas with Tom.

I had wanted to give Eileen plenty of notice, so that she could make other arrangements. I did not want her to spend Christmas on her own. Three days later I had a call from my aunt Angela to say that Eileen had rung her two or three times and was upset because I had 'spoken harshly' to her and was not inviting her for Christmas. I was flabbergasted by this; my conversation with Eileen had been entirely amicable. It was apparent that Eileen had not mentioned to Angela the reason I did not feel able to invite her for Christmas. Indeed, Angela was unaware that Morag was pregnant. Angela said she suspected that Eileen dreamt things which she then believed had actually occurred. This was something that I later became convinced was happening to my mother.

Angela presumably said that she would speak to me and this put Eileen in a tizzy. 30 minutes or so after Angela's call, a note from Eileen arrived in the post. She wrote:

Dear Anna and Michael,
    I'm very sorry if my words have been misconstrued by Angela. I have always been appreciative of everything you have done for me and would not have hurt you both for the world, however you must know me better than that, what more can I say.

I replied the next day saying that some wires appeared to have crossed and reiterated what I had said on the telephone. I informed her that a copy of my letter was being sent to Angela so that there could be no further misunderstanding. When writing to Angela I said that I could only assume that Eileen had forgotten the reason for her not being invited for Christmas, had then fretted about it and her imagination had run riot.

*

Weekly visits to my mother were continuing with nothing of interest occurring.

*

In mid-September I received a telephone call from Angela who informed me that there had been further problems regarding Eileen. The latter had rung my other aunt, June, and apparently told her that I was taking her to a hotel for Christmas! June wrote to me the following day reporting on two recent calls she had received. Eileen was worried that she was going away for Christmas, to where she hadn't a clue, but she wanted a bedroom on her own because she was a bad sleeper. She told June that she was unable to come to my house as Andrew's wife was expecting a baby and I was going to London for Christmas. June was aware of the actual situation because Angela had told her about my letter to Eileen. She said that it was all the more strange as Eileen read that letter to her and it bore little relation to her understanding of it. When June asked her if she had received another letter from me, she said she did not think so but thought that I had rung her. June told her that she would contact Angela to find out if there had been a change in the arrangements. On learning that there had not been, she called Eileen to tell her not to worry, she would be staying at home over Christmas. Eileen seemed relieved to hear this. June was, however, concerned about Eileen's confusion and asked me to inform the warden of the Christmas arrangements.

I had other worries at that time. Morag had just given birth, after only 25 weeks, and her baby was in a very precarious state. Tragically he only lived for ten days. I tried to help Andrew and Morag in practical ways, by making arrangements for the cremation and going with them to register the baby's birth and death at the same time. That, and the cremation service a few days later, have been the saddest days of my life.

*

Tom had to deal with our mother's shopping and hairdressing appointment on the week of my grandson's death. He told her of the news. By the time I saw her the following week, she had, of course, forgotten all about it.

Another sign of my mother's worsening mental condition was that she had become less concerned about her appearance. Her weekly visit to the hairdresser had been almost sacrosanct. Even when we used to take her away on holiday, she had to have her hair done, regardless of the location. Yet, by 2008, she would quite often be prepared to miss going, usually on the basis that she did not feel well, although I got the impression that that was just a pretext. This happened twice in October. On the second occasion she did not even pretend to be ill. She was due to spend the following weekend at Tom's house but did not want to go there either. When I got to her house she was up but not yet dressed. The clocks had gone back an hour two days earlier, but she was unaware of that. Clearly, the carers had not changed the clocks either.

During that week a security company was installing a new intruder alarm system which I had arranged in order to comply with the requirements of my mother's household insurers. To avoid any problems, Tom stayed in the house for a couple of nights. I went there for the day on the Friday when the installation was completed. I was there for almost seven and a half hours and returned home worn out. For anyone who has no experience of spending time with a relative with significant dementia problems, this may sound hyperbolic but, believe me, it becomes a strain after just half an hour.

There were no further problems with my mother in November. When I went to see her at the beginning of December, it had registered with her that Christmas was approaching. I suspect that the hairdresser had been talking to her about it.

She was then fretting about what to get people as presents. No sooner would I answer a question, she would ask another. I kept explaining to her that I was dealing with the matter, but she was unable to retain information for more than a second or two. Writing this now, I can see there appears to be a contradiction. If she had almost no short-term memory, how did she remember that it would soon be Christmas? I wish I knew the answer.

I think it was about this time that Anna and I arrived home one evening to find two telephone messages from Mother. She appeared to think that the female voice requesting her to leave a message was a real person answering the phone. She spoke to this woman at length, seeming to lose patience that she was getting no response. Her second call was similar to the first. She had probably forgotten having rung earlier.

*

Later that week I went to Eileen's flat for a meeting with a financial adviser from her bank. She had led me to think that the bank had requested the meeting, but I got the impression from the adviser (who, it transpired, was from the bank's private client department) that she had come following a request from Eileen at her branch for advice on available interest rates on savings accounts. Before the meeting, I had a brief look through Eileen's papers to give myself some idea of her financial affairs. The information I gleaned was, in some respects, expanded by the financial adviser and I subsequently prepared a note to provide both me and Eileen with a composite record. I wrote to her with a copy, pointing out that it was incomplete in several respects and that I would need to see all her papers to fill in the gaps.

At the meeting, the adviser had tried to convince Eileen that she should change her current account to a private client account where, for a fee of £25 a month, she would be able to telephone the bank for assistance, when required, and would obtain various benefits at no extra cost. Following the meeting, I read the bank's literature on the proposed account from which it was apparent that these benefits were mainly illusory. She would get worldwide travel insurance; this was not much use to an old woman who did not like spending a night away from her home, had not taken a holiday in many years and was so pusillanimous that, even when her husband was alive, the only foreign holiday she had taken was to the Republic of Ireland. She would also get AA breakdown cover and motor vehicle accident management cover; this for a woman who did not own a car and had never learned to drive. Then there was mobile phone insurance: she did not own a mobile phone. A card protection policy was also included in the package; this was not really a necessity for someone who only had one debit card and one credit card, with the latter rarely used. As an added inducement, the bank offered to include in the package her identity theft protection insurance, which it had previously persuaded her to take out at £6.99 a month. This for a woman who had never owned a computer and did not understand what the Internet was.

In my letter to her, I advised Eileen that she should stick with her existing current account. I went on to express my concern at the extent of her reliance on her bank for all investment advice. She had been with it all her adult life and the bulk of her funds were with it or an investment company owned by it. I explained to her that her bank did not provide independent financial advice and would, therefore, only recommend its own products or those of its subsidiaries. Consequently, she had too many eggs in one basket and, moreover, she had lost out in obtaining better returns which would have been available from other financial institutions. With regard to the first of these issues, I went on to explain that the world economy was going through a very difficult period with several major banks collapsing or having to be rescued by governments. To provide more confidence to UK investors, the British government was guaranteeing bank deposits up to £50,000 for each customer in any UK bank or building society. I suggested that, as a matter of prudence, it would be sensible to reduce the investments with her bank to £50,000. (Following the sale of her bungalow and downsizing to her flat, she was in a comfortable financial position.) I explained that it was open to her to take advice from a registered independent financial adviser, although that would involve her in either paying a fee or the IFA receiving commission from the investment company. Alternatively, I could help her in spreading her funds between her bank and other banks or building societies. (She was an unsophisticated woman and was only really interested in deposit accounts. Of course, in those days, it was possible to obtain attractive rates of interest from such investments.)

In the same letter I also mentioned another matter of concern to me. I had discovered that her other nephew, who had been jointly appointed with me under the enduring power of attorney, had moved to the Far East with his wife, apparently permanently. He had not bothered to inform me, and Eileen said she did not know his address. To make matters worse, he and I had also been appointed as her executors.

*

On the same day as posting my letter to Eileen, I sent off most of my mother's Christmas cards, which I had got her to sign the previous week. I also prepared a list of the presents she was giving to people. Anna would give her the list when she went to see her the next day, to stop her from worrying over the matter.

I did some Christmas shopping later in the week for both myself and for Mother. One of the items I bought, although not as a gift, was a pair of cordless headphones for Mother's use when she came to stay with us for Christmas. The intention was that she could wear them while watching TV. This meant that the volume could be adjusted on the headphones, so that she could hear the programmes, but it could stay at a normal level for the rest of us.

*

In mid-December I went to see Eileen to collect her financial papers and bring them home temporarily so that they could be put into a filing system. They were in such a mess that sorting them out was a long and tedious process.

Andrew and Morag went to Scotland to stay with her parents over Christmas. Sarah and Jonathan came to us. It was the first time he had spent Christmas with us, and it turned out to be a memorable one, although not entirely for reasons we might have wished.

I collected my mother on Christmas Eve, arriving at her house before 11:30 am. She had packed her bag but had not yet had breakfast. She then dithered for over one and a half hours before we could leave. That day she gave us a taste of what was to come. Sarah and Jonathan showed her their wedding photos. She did not recognise Morag from them or, indeed, remember ever having met her; she could also not remember the name of one of Tom's daughters. By the evening, she seemed surprised to learn that Jonathan was married to Sarah.

Sarah was woken at about 6:00 on Christmas morning by her grandmother calling out for a nurse. Sarah went into her room to find out what was wrong and found Mother standing up in the dark. She needed to go to the lavatory but could not find her way or locate a light switch. This was even though she had a lamp on the bedside cabinet and a light pull above her pillow. She had slept in that room on many occasions yet was totally disorientated.

Because of the tragic circumstances in September, we were, after all, able to have Eileen on Christmas Day. I collected her in the morning and, on arriving back home, she and Mother embarked on one of their talkathons.

After Christmas lunch, Sarah, Jonathan, Anna and I went out for a walk, leaving the two old ladies sitting on the sofa in front of the log fire. On our return, my mother informed me of what she considered to be the most amazing coincidence. She said that she had discovered that the lady sitting next to her was named Eileen Morris and that she was Mother's long-lost sister. Eileen was as bemused by this as the rest of us.

Eileen went home in the early evening and the rest of us watched some TV. The cordless headphones seemed to be a success. After a while, four of us had a game of Trivial Pursuit. Mother was asked if she wished to play but declined. Shortly afterwards she got up to go to the lavatory and, as she was leaving the room, let rip with a couple of very loud farts. She seemed wholly oblivious to this, probably because she could not hear them, while Jonathan and I tried to suppress a fit of the giggles. After she had been absent for about 15 minutes, Sarah went to find out whether she was alright. Shortly after, we heard my mother's raised voice. She had gone into the dining room and found the crockery, which had been used at lunch, stacked on the dining room table, where we had placed it after doing the washing-up, ready for use the next day. For some reason, this offended my mother who felt it should have been put back in the sideboard. She blamed Sarah for this outrage, telling her it was disgraceful and that she knew the people who owned the house as they were friends of her husband. Anna went out to pacify Mother who subsequently retired to bed. Jonathan remarked that one of his grandparents had suffered from dementia, but they were nowhere near as bad as my mother. The rest of us were quite shocked by her behaviour that day. It was far worse than the usual memory loss and confusion. I thought that some of it may have been caused by her having drunk more alcohol than she was accustomed to drinking. The change of surroundings also seemed to have played a part. Mother was very confused again on Boxing Day. Among other things, she had got it into her head that she was due to go home that day and had therefore packed her case. Anna and I thought that she would be less confused in her own home and so did not try to dissuade her. Sarah and I drove her home in the afternoon. That was the last Christmas she spent with us.

Chapter Twelve

2009

January was a dramatic month and was the start of a new chapter in my mother's life.

There was a very cold start to the year and, when I went to see Mother during the first week of January, the hairdresser rang to cancel her appointment as their water tank had frozen. On that visit Mother pointed to Sarah's wedding photograph and said: "The husband is odd looking, and she is a very silly girl." She had just spent Christmas with them yet appeared to have forgotten their names. It was also unclear whether she understood that Sarah was my daughter. That, of course, was attributable to the dementia, but I do not accept the same applied to the spiteful nature of the comments. Her dementia may have caused her to express views which she might, if mentally sound, have chosen to keep to herself in my presence, but there was no escaping the fact that she held those views. There was, moreover, no justification for either of them. Jonathan is a nice-looking guy, and Sarah is not silly...at least was not silly in front of her grandmother.

At that stage, although my mother's short-term memory was almost non-existent, her medium-term memory was still functioning to some extent. I think that she bore deep-seated grudges against certain people, including Sarah and me, although she could no longer remember the causes, real or imagined.

*

The next day I attended a meeting at Eileen's flat with a different financial adviser from her bank. Although I had not met this woman before, she was known to Eileen and had been the one who had advised on the investment of the surplus proceeds from the sale of Eileen's bungalow. The meeting was helpful as the adviser was able to clarify several matters for me. I brought home more papers and, after reading them, started work on a long letter to Eileen, summarising the points discussed both with the adviser and after she had left. For present purposes, only three are relevant. Firstly, as the rate of interest the bank was paying on Cash ISAs was comparatively low, it would have been sensible to transfer her ISAs to another fund manager. I agreed to investigate that for her. Secondly, as she was still unable to inform me of her other nephew's address in the Far East, or even whether he had gone to live there permanently, it was agreed that the most sensible course of action would be to revoke the existing power of attorney and to put in place new arrangements appointing her sister, Angela, and myself as joint and several attorneys. Unfortunately, since the original document was signed, a new system had been introduced on 1st October 2007 whereby Enduring Powers of Attorney were replaced by Lasting Powers of Attorney. The new system required two separate documents (one relating to property and financial matters, the other to health and welfare) and was more expensive. I said I would try to deal with these myself to save her legal fees. Thirdly, it was agreed that, whilst the situation regarding the powers of attorney was being sorted out, Eileen would sign letters authorising her bank, and a building society with which she had savings accounts, to provide me with any information I needed concerning her financial affairs. I enclosed the letters for her signature and return to me.

I completed and posted my letter to Eileen the next day. The same day our central heating and hot water boiler broke down. A heating engineer called round and advised us that it was incapable of repair and needed to be replaced. This could not have happened at a worse time as far as the weather was concerned. Fortunately, we had several electric heaters in the house and an immersion heater.

*

Three days later, on a Sunday, we received a telephone call from one of the carers to report that my mother's boiler was not working. She had left Mother in an armchair, covered with a blanket, in front of an electric heater. Anna and I drove round to find Mother sitting in her chair wholly unaware that there was a problem. We were unable to start the boiler and I rang British Gas, with whom she had a Home Care agreement, but was informed that they were unable to come out to her until Wednesday, even though I stressed that she was almost 85 and lived alone. I managed to arrange for a local heating engineer to come the following day. There was little point in taking her back to our house as we too were without a functioning boiler.

That evening I had a long telephone conversation with Tom in which I expressed my concern about Mother continuing to live on her own when she was incapable of dealing with any problem which arose. Consequently, I was, effectively, on 24-hour call. It was a difficult subject as Mother refused to accept that she could not manage. The problem was, however, about to be resolved.

The next morning, I arrived at Mother's at about 10:30 to meet the central heating engineer. Pamela was on duty that morning and had arrived shortly before me. She was unable to get into Mother's bedroom as the door was locked. As far as we were aware, Mother had not previously locked herself in. I had to hammer on the door and shout very loudly for several minutes before she heard me and understood why we could not enter. When she eventually opened the door, we could see that she was bruised in several places and the room looked as if it had been ransacked, with various pieces of furniture lying on the floor. She could offer no explanation for what had happened. Pamela and I concluded that my mother had got up to go to the bathroom in the night, had not been able to locate her bedside light, had become disorientated in the dark and had collided with the furniture. I rang her GP, arranged for a home visit that day and asked Pamela to dress Mother. Meanwhile, the heating engineer was able to fix the boiler on a temporary basis but advised that it needed to be replaced.

The GP arrived just after 1:00 pm and advised that the injuries were superficial. We agreed, however, that my mother ought to go into a local nursing home for a week or so and, in the meantime, I would try to get her boiler replaced. The doctor spoke to a nursing home and, after viewing it, I booked Mother in for eight days. The idea was sold to her on the basis that she would be going there for a short holiday while the problem with the boiler was sorted out. Subsequently, I helped her pack a case and drove her there. The next day I drove to her house again, this time to meet a heating engineer so that he could quote for installing a new boiler. I then visited Mother at the nursing home. She seemed happy.

A few days later, Anna and I called at the nursing home to see Mother on her birthday. I also had several telephone conversations with the care agency, the community psychiatric nurse, Social Services, the Department for Work and Pensions, the manager of the nursing home, and Tom. Most, and possibly all, of these conversations were concerned with her living arrangements after she left the nursing home.

It was now clear that Mother needed full-time care, although she strongly denied it. Several issues arose: firstly, the type of care; secondly, how the care should be funded; and, thirdly, where she would be based.

The first issue involved her either going into a care home or remaining in her own home, but with a carer living in permanently. The second option was not practicable. We did not think Mother was safe going up and down the stairs unaided; the staircase, moreover, was unsuited for a stairlift. Furthermore, there was no bathroom on the ground floor and so, if she were restricted to that floor, the property would have had to be adapted. In addition, it would not have been feasible to employ an individual carer as we would have had to arrange cover for when she (or he) had days off, went on holiday or was on sick leave. It would therefore have been necessary to use an agency which would have been very expensive. If one also took into account the fact that my mother would have continued to incur the usual expenses of living in her home, as well as the cost of feeding the carer, the total cost would probably have exceeded that of moving to a care home.

My mother was in the position of having to pay for the entirety of her care because her assets, excluding her home, comfortably exceeded the very low threshold (£23,250) set for local authority funding. I prepared schedules of all her investments from which it was immediately obvious that the total income they produced, even when combined with her State Pension, was nowhere near sufficient. We considered several means of paying for the cost of care but, unfortunately, there was no real alternative to selling her home. This was far from ideal at that time as the housing market was in the middle of a slump. Delaying a sale was not, however, a realistic option as we did not know how long the slump would last or, indeed, whether house prices would continue to fall.

The question of where Mother would be based did not take long to resolve. It was a matter of either a care home near me, or one near Tom. We researched homes in our respective areas but, as he lives in North London, those near him were significantly more expensive than the ones near me.

Before taking the step of putting my mother in a care home, to which she would have been strongly opposed, I felt it was necessary to obtain a care management assessment from a care officer at Hampshire County Council. I arranged a meeting with this officer while my mother was at the nursing home. This was initially at Mother's house and, from there, we visited the nursing home where he interviewed her. During the interview, my mother yet again demonstrated an unrealistic belief in her own abilities. For example, she informed the officer that she enjoyed cooking her dinner every day. She was also unaware of the other aspects of care being provided. She was unable to give her address or even to say what her house looked like. She thought she lived in a flat with a door that faced the neighbouring flat. This was very strange as she appeared to be describing Eileen's accommodation.

I was impressed by the depth of the assessment and the degree of urgency exhibited in its production. As part of the exercise, the officer judged whether my mother had the mental capacity to appreciate and understand the potential risks she would be facing on a daily basis if she was to return home. In addition to his own findings, he also obtained the views of her GP, her psychiatrist, the community psychiatric nurse, the deputy manager of the nursing home, and me. The report concluded:

The overwhelming evidence of a deterioration in Mrs Norman's mental state due to her vascular dementia means that her identified needs would be best met with 24-hour care to improve and maintain her quality of life and well-being. The family have been providing support and assistance since her diagnosis and feel that it is no longer a safe option for their mother to remain at home even with an increase in care. All the professionals agree that because of the level of confusion Mrs Norman experiences the only decision they can make in her best interest is a move to a home that would provide the correct level of support 24 hours a day.

This assessment meant that moving Mother to a care home was in compliance with the Mental Capacity Act.

Over the next few days I undertook a lot of research into prospective care homes, and Anna and I looked at several in our area. Tom did the same in his neck of the woods. Some of these were really depressing. You were sometimes greeted at reception with a distinct smell of urine. There were also cases of clearly disturbed residents wandering around and going uninvited into other residents' bedrooms. These homes were what are sometimes known as EMI residential homes, the initials standing for elderly, mentally impaired. We wished to avoid this type of place if at all possible. Some homes had two distinct sections: one for elderly residents who were not mentally ill, and the other for EMI residents. We got the impression that, even if Mother started off in the first section, it would not be long before she was moved to the second. We were fortunate in finding a non-EMI residential home, Prince's Manor, that was prepared to accept her, despite her dementia. The manager explained that that would not have been the case if Mother had been incontinent, violent or a 'wanderer'. Tom, Anna and I all liked the place and Mother spent a day there as a trial run. She seemed to have a pleasant day and passed muster with the management.

The next day, Anna and I drove to Mother's house where we packed some more of her clothes, plus some photographs, ornaments and other items to take to the care home. I also collected a month's worth of her medications from the pharmacy. After lunch we picked Mother up from the nursing home and drove her to Prince's Manor. She had forgotten going there the previous day, although she seemed to have some recollection later.

The following day I telephoned the care agency, Pamela, the pharmacy and the newsagent to let them know that my mother had moved into a care home and would not be returning.

Tom went to visit Mother two days after she had moved in to Prince's Manor and found her in a miserable mood. She did not understand what she was doing there and wanted to go home. He tried to explain the position to her, but it did not help. She said she might as well be dead. Tom was worried that the home might not be prepared to keep her.

I prepared a cash flow projection of Mother's finances to the end of March, as she could not afford to pay the care home's fees for long without selling her house. Indeed, there would be insufficient funds to pay the fees in April without selling one of her investments. Her medical insurance policy was due to expire at the end of that month and Tom and I decided not to renew it. The last annual premium was almost £1,250, and we took the view that renewal was a waste of money for two reasons. Firstly, any hospital admission at her age was likely to be for an emergency, and the policy would probably not apply. Secondly, her mental state was such that she would be unlikely to appreciate the difference between an NHS hospital and a private one.

There was a lot of other work for me to do regarding my mother's financial affairs. This included arranging for all the investment companies, who had been writing to her home address, to send everything to my address in future; obtaining a Council Tax exemption for the period her house would be unoccupied; applying for the higher rate of Attendance Allowance from the Department for Work and Pensions (which was then £70.35 a week, approximately only 11% of the care home fees, but better than nothing); arranging to have her antique furniture, jewellery, and various other possessions valued; restoring the income distribution for three of her ISAs; closing her bank account and moving it to my bank; dealing with her household insurers regarding the fact that her house was now unoccupied; and contacting her utilities suppliers.

On one of the occasions I visited my mother's house at this time, I spoke to her neighbour (the one for whom she had developed an unreasonable dislike), to explain that she had had to go into a care home. He was not surprised and, during our conversation, mentioned an incident involving her car of which I had been wholly unaware. Before she had been prevented from driving, she had managed to partially demolish the low brick wall separating her front garden from her neighbour's.

He thought she had reversed into it whilst backing out of her garage. To have done this, she must have steered very sharply to the left while reversing at great speed. It almost beggars belief. I do not know exactly when this happened, but it must have been at a time when she was still in control of her finances as I never saw any evidence of an insurance claim or a payment having been made. I also never saw any sign of damage to the wall or to the car. She must have had repairs to both carried out very promptly so that neither Tom nor I would discover what had happened. I can only assume that this had occurred before her dementia arose or, at least, before it was diagnosed.

My mother was unaware that she would not be returning to her home. She would have been devastated if she had known. As far as she was concerned, she was only at the care home for a short while until she recovered. She thought she was in hospital. For several weeks following her arrival, she would occasionally have her bag packed in the morning, thinking she would be taken home that day. At other times, when she was in a sunnier mood, she would think she was on a cruise and would ask members of staff when the ship would next be docking. This delusion persisted for several months.

Mother did have occasions of comparative lucidity. Late one evening, in early February, I received a telephone call from Tom reporting on a call he had just had from her. She was angry and blaming the two of us for putting her in the home. He had been unable to pacify her and was upset by the conversation. Fortunately, she had forgotten all about her call by the next day when Anna and I went to see her. We had been to her house beforehand to carry out a few jobs, including emptying her fridge/freezer.

The following week Anna and I went back to the house, where we were joined by Tom. We had a meeting with a local estate agent with a view to selling the place. Half an hour later we had another meeting, this time with a representative of a well-known auction house, to obtain a valuation of Mother's furniture, paintings and *objets d'art*. We were disappointed by his view of the prices we might obtain at auction; some of the pieces were worth considerably less than she had led us to believe.

The three of us had lunch together before visiting Mother. She was miserable and very confused. The extent of her confusion can be illustrated by a story she told us of Jack Lister, an old friend of our parents, turning up at her house about a week earlier. He had come to see her, and our father was jealous. Pausing here. Our father had died almost 25 years earlier, at the age of 82. If I recall correctly, Jack had not been much younger than him, and nothing had been heard of Jack for many years. He was almost certainly dead too. This was the first of several sightings of Jack that we heard about over the next few months. We began to suspect that, in the distant past, Mother had harboured a secret infatuation.

It may have been on this occasion that we learned that Mother's watch had gone missing. This was presumably the one that Tom and I had bought to replace the earlier one she had lost.

*

Further problems now arose with Eileen. I had written to her bank in January, explaining that my aunt had asked me to assist her in managing her financial affairs, and requesting information or clarification of seven separate matters. With that letter I enclosed the letter from Eileen authorising them to provide me with whatever information I needed. Unfortunately, someone at the bank had misunderstood the letter of authority as being a request by Eileen for me to be a signatory on her account. The letter had been unambiguous. There had been no such request. They wrote to me (with a copy to my aunt) explaining that it would be necessary for us both to sign an application form. They went on to say that the information I had requested would be sent to my aunt. I was furious and rang the bank. After a while they connected me to the branch manager, who had not even seen my letter. She explained that it would have gone to a service centre. The branch was aware that I was assisting my aunt and, indeed, that she needed help. The manager gave me the information I needed. I was worried, however, that Eileen might have been alarmed by the bank's letter into believing that I was trying to take control of her account. What happened next suggests that my concern was justified.

Two weeks later I had a telephone call from Christine, a personal banker in Eileen's local branch. She informed me that my aunt had gone into the branch that morning and had told her that she did not understand why she needed a power of attorney, did not want one and was frightened (although it was unclear of what). Christine, who had not met Eileen before, had agreed to ring me later that day. She proposed that I should attend a meeting at the bank, with Eileen, in an attempt to clear matters up.

The next day I spoke to my aunt Angela and followed this up with a letter. After recounting the telephone call from the bank, I continued:

Frankly, I am really annoyed about this as it demonstrates that, despite my best efforts to help Eileen, she does not appreciate or understand what I am doing and, even worse, does not trust me. If she did, why not speak to me rather than to a bank official she has never previously met? This, combined with Eileen's bizarre conduct last year, has convinced me that it would sensible to stop trying to assist her with her financial affairs. If I carry on, there is a risk that I am going to be accused of dishonesty. It was in order to avoid that risk that I have taken the trouble to keep her fully informed in writing. Unfortunately, her mental state seems to be worse than I thought. The situation is not helped by [her bank] treating my request for information as a request to be a signatory on her account.

Having put Eileen's papers in order, I will return them to her during the next few days. I will also give her a note of outstanding matters she can discuss with the bank. I will inform her that, in view of the call I received from the bank and the demands on my time in dealing with my mother's affairs, I do not feel able to assist her any longer. As I mentioned to you over the telephone, I intend to speak tomorrow to the lady at Social Services, who contacted me some time ago, to let her know what is happening and to ask her to keep Eileen's mental capacity under review. In addition, I will speak to the bank to inform them that I will no longer be involved.

The next day I rang Christine, telling her that I had been concerned by her call and had spoken to another of my aunts who had reminded me that it was the bank who had suggested to Eileen that she should execute a power of attorney. Christine then expanded on what had happened. Eileen had gone in to withdraw some cash and had started telling the cashier that she was worried about her power of attorney. The cashier did not think it was appropriate to hold this discussion in public, so she called over Christine who took Eileen into an office. She asked Eileen if it would help if they got on the phone to me, but Eileen did not want to speak to me. It was left on the basis that Christine would ring me later. I explained that I felt that I could no longer assist Eileen with her financial affairs as it appeared that she did not trust me fully. I would therefore return Eileen's papers that afternoon.

Next, I rang the Adult Mental Health Services for Eileen's area. The community nurse who had spoken to me a year or two earlier was no longer there, but I was able to speak to the team leader, Alan. I explained Eileen's situation to him and said that I felt that it was necessary for her mental health to be monitored. Alan was very helpful, offering to look up Eileen's records and ring me back. He did so promptly, informing me that Pat, one of his community workers, saw Eileen about every two weeks. She had rung Eileen to see her in two days' time and almost the first thing that Eileen had mentioned to her was the power of attorney. Alan said he would accompany Pat on that visit and would contact me afterwards.

The same afternoon I went to see Eileen and returned her papers. I had put them in chronological order and placed them in a concertina file for which I had prepared an index. Eileen seemed unable to concentrate. She could not find any of the letters that I had sent her or any of the recent correspondence from her bank. She could not even remember receiving my letters. She said she could not recall making a power of attorney and seemed surprised that she had done so several years ago. I gained the impression that she was worried about it because she associated my mother's power of attorney with Mother going into a care home. I was surprised about the large amount of unfiled correspondence tucked away in various places as I had thought that I had been given all material documents. She said that she had not had time to sort it out. (She had, in fact, had plenty of time as she did very little all day and rarely left the confines of her building.) I gave her some notes on her financial position and stressed that she should read them carefully and act on them. I was fairly confident that she would do very little, if anything.

After I had got home, Eileen rang me twice, asking whether I had taken her bank statements folder with me. I told her both times that I had not taken anything away with me that day and, indeed, had never had that folder.

*

The next day I had a meeting at my mother's house with the owner of an antiques business who had valued her furniture several years earlier for insurance purposes. He was interested in buying several items. A few days later he sent me an offer which I was able to compare with the recent valuation for auction purposes. In the event, some pieces were sold to the dealer, some went to auction, and some were bought by Tom and me and my children. I emptied Mother's safe, which principally contained her jewellery, and took the contents home with me together with some silverware.

The following morning, I took the jewellery to be valued. From there I went to see my mother. She was not in the mood for talking. I also telephoned the nursing home, where Mother stayed for a short while before moving into the care home, to see if she had left her watch there. It seemed she had not. At least she was not accusing Sarah of having stolen it.

Towards the end of February, Tom and I went to see Mother. She was in a foul mood and declined to come out for lunch with us. She made it clear that she did not like it at the home and felt that we had abandoned her. The two of us went out for a pub lunch before returning to Prince's Manor for a meeting with the manager. Before that, we saw Mother again. She was in a far better mood, having had lunch in the communal dining room. The manager informed us that the home was happy to keep Mother there. The staff thought she was settling in quite well and the view was expressed that she was saving up the misery for her sons.

A week later Anna, Sarah (who had come for the day) and I drove to the care home. Tom was already there, and we all went out for lunch with Mother. I have nothing in my diary to indicate there were any problems that day. I do remember, however, that during this period she would often enquire about her house and we would say that we were keeping an eye on it. We made no mention of it going on the market, or of the disposal of her furniture. She persisted in the apparent belief that she was only in her current accommodation on a temporary basis pending a return to her own house. We made no attempt to disabuse her of that idea.

Earlier in the day I had collected the jewellery from the valuers. Tom and I agreed that I would retain it for the time being until we decided what to do with it. Some of the pieces were quite valuable, and it would not have been sensible for Mother to have them with her. She did have her wedding, engagement and eternity rings (the latter two being valuable items) but these were permanently on her ring finger and would be very difficult to remove. I had the jewellery added to my household policy and the additional premium subsequently debited to her account.

A few days later, Anna and I removed the remaining silverware from Mother's house, so that it could be valued. Tom and I later sold most of it, although we bought a few pieces ourselves.

My mother's house went on the market in late March. In preparation for that, Anna and I spent several hours cleaning the place. Although Tom was dealing with the sale of the house, the estate agents sent the draft sale particulars to me for approval. I am not a fan of estate agents, and these ones did nothing to change my opinion, as can be seen from the following paragraph taken from my reply:

It appears that you may not have been informed that you should be liaising with my brother, Tom, regarding the proposed sale of the property, rather than with me. I have, however, read the draft and am returning one copy amended in red. The corrections are so numerous that I can but assume that it was not checked before leaving your office. Of particular concern is the misspelling of the name of the road on two of the three occasions it is mentioned and of the description of the front garden as being 'laid mainly to lawn' when it is, in fact, paved.

I continued to see my mother on a weekly basis and there were no untoward incidents for a while. Life became a little easier for me after her admission to the care home. I no longer had to take her to the hairdresser, thereby avoiding the aggravation of trying to ensure she was ready in time. Moreover, although I was still responsible for dealing with her finances, several of the individual items of expenditure were removed when she left her house. Most importantly, I knew she was receiving 24-hour care, which was a weight off my mind.

*

In early April I received four telephone calls from Eileen, in about eight days, in which she kept on about a power of attorney. She had apparently been warned about them by her friend's sister who used to work in a solicitors' office. In Eileen's eyes, that made her an expert on the subject.

*

At the end of May, Anna and I spent about eight and a half hours at Mother's house, where we were joined by Tom for a large part of that time. We cleared out a load of her clothes and other items from several rooms. Most of the clothes were either given to charity or thrown away. It was apparent that Mother had not got rid of any clothes for very many years. We brought home anything that she might still have been able to wear. I also retrieved a lot of old photographs, which I subsequently put in some sort of order, before taking them to the care home. They proved useful for a while, as being something to talk to her about since her long-term memory was still relatively unimpaired.

In early June, Sarah gave birth to her first child, a daughter. This news did not appear of interest to my mother and I suspect that, at that stage, she could not even remember Sarah.

Contracts were due to be exchanged in mid-June for the sale of Mother's house. This necessitated several more sessions there, clearing out stuff, including yet more clothes, and cleaning. On one of those visits we wrapped, and removed for valuation, her collection of ivory and semi-precious stone carvings. In the event, exchange of contracts was delayed.

On one of my visits to the care home, I was concerned to see that a bottle of *eau de toilette* and a bottle of perfume were missing from my mother's room. This strengthened my view that we should avoid taking anything of value there. In fairness to the place, I think this was the only occasion when I suspected theft had occurred. There were several subsequent times when items of clothing had gone missing, but these probably went astray in the laundry and ended up in another resident's room.

A few days later, Tom and I took Mother out to lunch at a local garden centre. She was very bad on her feet and had to be helped out of the car and supported on the short walk from the car park to the restaurant. Progress was painfully slow. I also remember that she disappeared to the lavatory and was there for a worryingly long time. When we got her back to the care home, we managed to persuade her to have her hair done in the salon there. She had been refusing to go, having taken what appeared to be an irrational dislike to the hairdresser. Consequently, her hair was a mess

At the beginning of July, my mother's furniture was moved out of her house. I think that Tom had already removed the items he was having. As for the rest of the furniture being retained, I decided to use a specialist removal firm recommended to me by the antiques dealer who was buying some of it. His stuff was removed first. When the removers returned, they packed the items to come to me, including things to be sold at auction, plus a few smaller pieces to go in my mother's room at the care home. We called at the care home first. Despite having informed the manager two days earlier of the furniture that I would be replacing, she had not ensured that it had been removed by the time we arrived. The process therefore took a little longer than it should have done. My mother did not appear to understand what was happening and was demonstrably angry with me for the disruption. I thought that she would have been pleased to have some of her own furniture in her room, but she was not. Thinking about it now, I wonder if the cause of her anger was the realisation that her stay at the home was unlikely to be temporary.

I went to see her again six days later, to take her a framed photograph of my father, plus a box of books from her house to go in the care home's small library. My mother had always enjoyed reading fiction but, sadly, had not been capable of doing so for a while. She was unable to absorb what was in front of her. She did not, however, appear to realise that. When, in attempts to make conversation, I would ask her what she had been up to recently, she would come out with a list of activities such as reading, cleaning her room, cooking and even gardening. Her wilder flights of fancy included painting and working on tapestries. She would point to a tapestry on the wall, or the cover on a footstool, which she had embroidered about 50 years earlier and tell me that she had just completed it. Sometimes, probably because of her poor eyesight, she would refer to the tapestry as a painting she had done. Her portrait, painted by the art master in my primary school when my mother had been about 32, hung on a wall in her room, and she claimed, on occasion, to have painted it herself. The reality was that she did almost nothing all day except sit in an armchair in her room, or in the communal lounge, eat her meals, and sometimes sit in front of the television, albeit she was incapable of understanding what she was watching, even if she had been able to hear it.

In mid-July, Anna and I drove to Mother's house to remove a few minor items, and to meet an electrician who carried out some remedial work. From there, we went to see Mother for an hour. She was in a cheerful mood. A few days later, a house clearance firm removed from her house what was left of her possessions. These were the items that nobody wanted. She would have been very upset if she had known. They included a pair of large free-standing mahogany wardrobes for which there was apparently no longer any demand. It was all rather sad.

At the start of the following week I was busy dealing with the disposal of some of Mother's stuff. Some items of comparatively low value had gone to a lesser auction house for sale. The receipt for the goods delivered there failed to record about half of the items. I had to call at the auction rooms to sort out the confusion. I took the collection of ivory and semi-precious carvings to a superior firm of auctioneers (the ones who had provided a valuation guide for the antique furniture) but, before doing so, I had to unwrap each item, photograph it, and re-wrap it, which was a monotonous task. I also took in a couple of paintings. In addition, I arranged for a local charity to call to collect boxes of books and sacks of Mother's clothes, bed linen and towels.

Sarah, Jon and their baby daughter, Millie, came to stay for a few days and, during that time, the five of us went to see my mother. As I went in, I told her that we'd brought my granddaughter to see her. She then saw Sarah and said that she could see the likeness to me. She simply had not recognised Sarah and thought that she was the granddaughter. That was flattering! When Jon appeared with Millie, Mother was very puzzled as to whose baby Millie was. At various times she appeared to think that Anna and I were the parents. So, in the space of a few minutes, I went from being Sarah's grandfather to Millie's father.

Exchange of contracts for the sale of Mother's house eventually took place at the end of July. In anticipation of completion, I had to arrange for investment of the proceeds of sale. In those days very attractive returns were available for fixed-term bonds, and I eventually (after completion in mid-August) split the proceeds between nine different banks or building societies. The procedure was complicated by virtue of the investments being made under a power of attorney. As I have already observed, the staff in banks and building societies are often not sufficiently familiar with powers of attorney, which can prove frustrating. It was further complicated by there being joint attorneys. This meant that every time I initiated the opening of an account, which included completing an application form, registering the power of attorney with the financial institution and proving my identity, Tom would have to visit the branch of the same institution local to him, sign the same form, and prove his identity. With the benefit of hindsight, the power should have been prepared on a joint and several basis. Thus, instead of everything having to be done together, one attorney is entitled to act separately from the other. This is more flexible and, therefore, often quicker.

At the beginning of August, there was a garden party at the care home. Anna and I arrived in the afternoon to find Mother still in bed and in a miserable mood. She maintained that she was ill, although there was nothing physically wrong with her. She was, however, aware that she could not remember much, and it was worrying her. This was a very rare instance of her acknowledging that she had a memory problem. Tom and Ruth arrived about 30 minutes after us and, between us, we managed to persuade Mother to get up. Once she was downstairs, she seemed quite happy. I think that this was the only time Ruth visited the care home in all the years Mother lived there. Neither would have claimed to have been the other's greatest fan.

Anna and I went to my mother's house again on 6th August and did a couple of hours' cleaning. We then took some of her clothes to a local dressmaker to be let out. She had been putting on a lot of weight since moving into the care home; she was eating well and getting almost no exercise.

A few days later we went to see Mother, taking with us a couple of skirts Anna had bought for her. She was still not dressed at 11:40 and was clearly depressed. We also learned that she needed various other clothes because some of the items she had taken with her no longer fitted. From there we drove to her house, finished off the cleaning and took the meter readings. After leaving, we dropped off the keys at the estate agents.

The next morning Anna went out to buy more clothes for my mother and I took them to her in the afternoon.

My cousin Maurice and his Japanese wife, Keiko, were visiting the UK in August. Maurice was only a few years younger than my mother but had retained all his marbles. He and Keiko were fond of her, and she had stayed with them a few years earlier at their home in Florida. They had also stayed at her house. They contacted me to say they would like to see her whilst in England. They were not deterred by my warning that she would probably not remember them. Anna and I met them at the station about noon one day and, from there, drove to the care home to collect Mother. We went out for lunch at a pleasant restaurant and, although everyone seemed to enjoy themselves, it was clear that my mother did not know who they were. They must have been dismayed to see how badly she had deteriorated since they had last seen her.

Nothing of interest occurred regarding my mother over the next few weeks, apart from the auctioneers informing me that they would be unable to sell quite a lot of the ivory carvings as the latter were insufficiently old. It had become illegal to sell ivory that did not pre-date 1947. It was therefore returned to me and I had difficulty in even giving it away. Tom had two or three small pieces but nobody else in the family wanted it. Regardless of the ethical issues, some of it was hideous and I do not know what persuaded my parents to buy it.

*

In the first half of October, I received a telephone call from someone who described himself as a senior wealth planning manager at Eileen's bank. He told me that he had had a meeting with my aunt at her flat and had observed that she had a very poor short-term memory. He had suggested to her that it would be sensible if he discussed his investment proposals with a family member. She had given him my name. I said that I was reluctant to become involved and explained why. The adviser went on to say that a fixed-term bond had just matured, and the proceeds had been transferred to my aunt's basic savings account. He had been discussing with her what to do with the proceeds. It was apparent to him that her income exceeded her outgoings. He accepted my point that she could obtain a better return on fixed-rate investments elsewhere. Having obtained from him the current position on her investments, I asked him to take no further action for the time being so that I could consider what to do. Briefly, Eileen had about £70,000 with her bank, sitting in a combination of a current account and savings accounts, earning very little interest. In addition, she had three investments with a wholly-owned subsidiary of the bank that were not performing well. Their value at that time was just over £91,000.

Following that conversation, I rang Angela to discuss it with her. It was obvious that Eileen was incapable of managing her finances and was totally reliant on her bank. Their track record was far from impressive. Apart from the fact that her money could have been working a lot harder for her, I was critical of the bank for putting her into a substantial investment in which, although the capital was protected, the funds were tied up for six years. This was hardly appropriate for a woman of over 80. Angela wanted me to help Eileen with her financial affairs but understood my reluctance to get involved again. I indicated that it would be a lot easier if

I were to do so under a power of attorney with Angela as my co-attorney. Eileen would need to be persuaded to sign two lasting powers of attorney but, in the meantime, I would try to assist her without them.

I have diary notes for 13th October showing that I had several telephone conversations that day with Eileen and her bank. In one of those conversations I learned that the bank had placed almost £40,000 of her money on a six-month deposit at the less than generous rate of 2% per annum. This had been done without her authority and I persuaded them to close that account and to place the funds in her easy access deposit account. Two days later I rang Eileen to discuss placing £50,000 with another financial institution which would pay a significantly higher rate of interest. She was agreeable to this and I subsequently arranged for a representative of a well-known building society to meet me at Eileen's flat a week later. That meeting was subsequently put back a week.

*

The following week Tom and I collected our mother from her care home and took her out to lunch. She was by now very lame and I thought she needed a Zimmer frame to get about as a walking stick was insufficient.

*

Before seeing Eileen next, I prepared the two requisite forms of lasting power of attorney, together with a deed revoking the earlier power. I also prepared a codicil to Eileen's will appointing Angela as my co-executor in place of the nephew who had moved abroad. In the meantime, Eileen had heard from him with his new address.

On 24th October, I went to see Eileen in the morning as I wanted to ensure that there were sufficient funds in her current account to meet a cheque drawn in favour of the building society. I took with me a letter authorising her bank to transfer £45,000 from her instant access account. She signed it and I posted it immediately after leaving her flat. Before doing so, I again explained to her why it was sensible to move some funds away from her bank and discussed with her the desirability of making a fresh power of attorney with Angela and me acting jointly and severally. She said she thought that we were already appointed as attorneys. It was apparent that she had forgotten the problems caused by her other nephew having left the country, and the fuss she had caused earlier in the year in the bank.

On 29th October, I drove to Eileen's for the meeting with the representative of the building society. Before she arrived, we rang Eileen's bank to ensure that the funds had been transferred to her current account. We were told that they had not been, but that it would be done that day and that, if there were any problems, they would ring back. The lady from the building society arrived with a colleague and, after going through the formalities to open a one-year bond, she left with Eileen's cheque for £50,000.

The following Wednesday there was a minor disaster. Eileen received letters from her bank and the building society informing her that the cheque had been dishonoured. Clearly the bank had yet again demonstrated its incompetence and had failed to transfer the requisite funds. Eileen rang me in a panic, not understanding what was going on and wondering what had happened to her money. I explained to her what I assumed had occurred and that she should ring the bank to obtain clarification. She said she wished she had never touched the money in the first place. About an hour later I received a call from the branch. Eileen had gone there and was in a flap. They had persuaded her to leave the funds with them and to invest them in a two-year bond at 4%. This was less than the building society was paying. I let Eileen know that I was fed up and was not prepared to be involved any longer.

I rang the building society to apologise for what had happened and then informed Angela by email. Angela replied that evening, telling me that she had rung Eileen to explain how frustrating it was for me to put in a lot of effort to help her with her investments only to learn that she had reinvested funds with her bank. Eileen had told her that she wanted to remain with her bank as it was convenient for where she lived. (This was, of course, illogical as I had merely been trying to place some funds in a building society fixed-term bond; it did not matter where the society was situated.) Angela also raised with her the power of attorney, only to be told by Eileen that she thought Angela and I were already her attorneys. After explaining that that was not the case and why it was important for Eileen to make a decision, Angela asked her if she would accept herself and me as her attorneys. Eileen replied, "I will have to think about that." Later in the conversation, Angela again asked the same question. Eileen reverted to saying that she thought we already were her attorneys. Angela gave up at that stage. Eileen said she did not want to upset me and would ring me the following day. Angela told me that she fully understood how frustrating it was for me; her conversation with Eileen was like talking to a child. She also told me that, during the conversation, she had informed Eileen that June and her husband had appointed their daughter as their attorney, just in case any problems arose, and that Angela and Roy would be appointing their son as theirs. Eileen's response was to the effect that she did not have dementia.

The following day I emailed Angela.

Anna and I have discussed what to do about Eileen. It is obvious that she is not able to manage her affairs properly. This is why [her bank] have been uneasy for some years in advising her. I saw some reports that their previous financial adviser wrote to Eileen advising that it would be desirable for a family member to be involved. When this happens, Eileen mentions my name and I get sucked in, spend a lot of time and achieve very little. She agrees to do something but either then forgets or can't be bothered. There is very little I can do for her without a power of attorney as I have no legal authority to act on her behalf.

Although I am fed up, Anna and I are concerned at her vulnerability to being conned out of her assets. There is also a concern that, unless the nettle is grasped now, it could be very messy and expensive if she does get significantly worse and there is no PoA in place. Brenda, the Kingsley Wood warden, expressed the view to me some time ago that she thought Eileen would go to pieces if she did not have Beryl to rely upon.

It seems to me that the best course of action might be if you and I were to see her together and attempt to persuade her to sign a PoA. She knows perfectly well that she has a very poor memory (which is why she writes so much down) and that she gets confused. We've all heard the reference to 'heptatic confusion' many times. There is no need to mention the 'D' word. Provided we assure her that we won't be rushing her off to a care home, I think she is likely to agree, especially as she seems to be under the impression that there is already a power in place. It is, I think, important to

*strike while the iron is hot, and we could take with us the
two PoAs that I have prepared and try to get them signed
and witnessed on the same day. I could attempt to arrange
for Brenda to be on standby with another witness.*

*I appreciate that it is a long way for you to come but
Anna and I would be delighted if you and Roy could stay
with us for a couple of nights. We could show you around
the area and take you to see my mother if you wanted.*

What do you think?

Angela replied the next day. She informed me that Eileen had
rung her that morning and seemed in a very pleasant mood. She
told Angela that I was going to see her to discuss her finances as,
although she could manage her day-to-day matters, she did get
panicky over her investments. Angela accepted my invitation to
stay and said that she would very much like to see my mother.

Eileen's idea that I was going to visit her to discuss her
finances was a figment of her imagination.

I was out for much of the day. When I returned home, Anna
reported that Eileen had telephoned in the morning to say that
she was now unhappy with the investment with her bank. Anna
took the opportunity of explaining to her that, although I was
prepared to assist her, there was not much I could do unless I
was acting under a power of attorney.

I returned Eileen's call in the late afternoon. She could not
remember what she had called about. When I prompted her that
I understood that she was unhappy about the investment, she
started on about the investment with the building society and
that it was inconvenient to go to their offices! She appeared to be
unaware that the reason for her problems earlier in the week was
that the bank had bounced her cheque. She was very confused.
I made it clear that I was annoyed at my time and that of the

building society having been wasted and at her asking for advice and then ignoring it.

I emailed Angela to inform her of these developments, saying that my patience had now been exhausted. I mentioned that I proposed to avoid Eileen until we saw her together. Finally, I suggested some dates for Angela and Roy to visit.

Angela confirmed that the proposed dates were convenient. She reiterated that she could understand my frustration. She said that she had had a call from June to ask if she was unwell. Eileen had rung June to say that Angela had been crying during their telephone conversation. I told Angela that Eileen had said the same thing to me but that I had not wanted to mention it before in case it had been true. It was another figment of Eileen's imagination.

A few days later Eileen rang me regarding the two-year bond she had been persuaded to take out with her bank. She now did not want it and, after a couple of telephone conversations with the bank, I was able to get it cancelled.

During that week I spent a lot of time reorganising the files containing her financial papers. Her investments produced a surprising amount of paperwork.

*

When I next went to see my mother, she was in a miserable mood and her hair looked terrible. She had had it washed by a carer under the shower, because it was dirty, and it looked lank. She had not been to the hairdresser for several weeks. I later rang the care home manager to ask her to reserve the meeting room for 23rd November as I would be bringing guests to see my mother. I also asked her to ensure that my mother went to the hairdresser.

*

In preparation for the visit to Eileen on 23rd November, I rang her to let her know that I would be coming that day and bringing Angela and Roy. She made a note of it. I also spoke to Alan of the Adult Mental Health Services to see if he would act as a certificate provider in respect of the two lasting powers of attorney that I was hoping Eileen would be signing. It is a requirement that a suitable person (such as a registered healthcare professional) certifies that the person granting a lasting power of attorney understands the document and has not been put under any pressure to sign it. He agreed to act, and I subsequently wrote him a long explanatory letter.

*

When I went to see my mother that week, she was in a reasonably happy mood. That was a small mercy. She was also in a good mood when I went to see her three days later with Angela and Roy. Rather surprisingly she remembered Angela, even though they had not seen one another for many years. She did not remember Roy. Angela, in an attempt to make conversation, mentioned my regular visits to the home. My mother responded that I only went rarely. I was not bothered by that, attributing it to the fact that her short-term memory was such that she would probably not have been able to remember if she had had a visitor a few hours earlier. I reminded her that this was my third visit in ten days. What did upset me was, after Angela mentioned Tom, Mother said that he visited frequently. He was, in fact, going less often than I did. Angela was aware that Tom was her sister's favourite, but it was apparent, from a conversation we had later, that she was surprised by the blatancy of the favouritism.

*

The next day, Sunday, I took Angela and Roy to see Eileen, who was in good form. She willingly signed the powers of attorney in the presence of a witness. After leaving her, we drove to the local hospital to drop off the two documents for Alan, who subsequently went to see Eileen in his role as certificate provider.

Angela and Roy left the following morning. Angela rang me later in the day to tell me that Eileen had left some unpleasant messages on her answering machine the previous morning before meeting with us. That was bizarre as Eileen had been in a happy mood when we were there.

*

In late 2009 I changed my investment managers and, at the same time, under the power of attorney, moved Mother's investments to the same company. These investments did not include the various fixed-term bonds with banks and building societies, which comprised the bulk of her assets, some of which I had renewed since originally taking them out. As the bonds matured over the next couple of years I transferred the funds to the new managers. They had to re-invest the proceeds as interest rates on bonds had fallen. It was necessary to manage her funds on the basis that sufficient income would be produced to pay the care home fees each month but, at the same time, to grow the capital, in so far as that was possible, as the liability for fees might continue for another ten years or more. She was approaching her 86th birthday but came from a family whose members were generally long-lived. So, skilful management of her finances was necessary. My mother was blissfully unaware of the basis on which she was living in the care home. If she had known of the cost she would have been horrified, albeit for a minute or two, after which she would have forgotten.

At the end of November, I wrote to various people on my mother's Christmas card list explaining her situation and that she would not in future be sending cards. There was no point in continuing to exchange seasonal greetings with people of whom she had no recollection.

A few days later I went to see my mother. On the way there, I collected her wedding photograph which I had had reframed for her. She was in a horrible mood, possibly because I had persuaded her to have her hair done. It seemed that she saved her unpleasantness up for my visits and was trying to make me feel guilty for her situation. At one stage she said that she thought that strangers were nicer to her than her own family were. I thought she was suffering from depression and spoke to the manageress about it. She said she would have a word with the doctor.

In mid-December, Anna and I went to see Mother, and Tom joined us. We stayed about one and a half hours. It was much easier when there were others present as Mother was generally in a better mood. Afterwards, the three of us went out to lunch. The days of my mother eating out had gone. She would occasionally be taken on a brief local outing, as part of a small group from the home, by some carers. Apart from that, she was confined to barracks. She was neither mentally nor physically fit enough to be allowed out.

*

A few days before Christmas, Anna and I went to see Eileen, and took with us a Christmas card and her presents. The two of us were spending the holiday with Andrew and Morag at their flat in south London. Morag was pregnant, with the baby due in early January. They wanted to be near their hospital just in case.

*

On 23rd December, Tom and I went to see our mother. She was befuddled, and it took a carer a long time to get her dressed. This meant that Tom and I had to hang around elsewhere whilst this took place. She did not complete dressing much before her lunchtime. As a consequence, we were only able to see her briefly.

Christmas that year was the first one in many years when we did not have my mother with us. Cruel as it might sound, we had a jollier time without her.

Chapter Thirteen

2010

At the start of the year I registered Eileen's lasting power of attorney relating to financial and property affairs. Angela and I decided not to register the one concerning health and welfare at that stage in case it caused Eileen to worry we were going to pack her off to a care home.

*

A new member of the family arrived in early January, Andrew and Morag having produced a daughter, Emily. Thus, the problems I was getting from two old women were, to some extent, counterbalanced by the pleasures derived from a baby girl.

During January I received a call from the manager of Prince's Manor informing me that a room had become available on the ground floor. Mother's current room was on the first floor and, although it had a good view over open countryside, she had to use the lift as she was incapable of managing the stairs. She also had to walk to the lift using her Zimmer frame. She was paying £695 a week; the ground floor room was £30 a week more. Anna and I went to look at it when visiting Mother, and Tom did so later in the week. We all thought she should move, which she did shortly afterwards.

There was considerable debate at that time over Mother's weight. It had started to increase during the two years or so before moving into the care home. However, since moving there, her weight had rocketed. As I have already said, she used to be no more than five feet tall in her bare feet. As she got older, she had shrunk a bit. She had been truly petite, with a dress size of only eight. After a year at the home, this had doubled owing to a combination of eating well, albeit not particularly healthily, and an almost total lack of exercise. The latter was not due to neglect but to her increasing lameness. She was in a vicious circle: the fatter she got, the less mobile she became, and the lack of mobility caused her to become fatter still. Tom and I were concerned about her deteriorating condition and we spoke to the manager about it. The latter's view was that, as eating was one of the few pleasures left to our mother, it would be a shame to deprive her of that. Our concern was that she might eventually get so fat that she would be unable to move, even with a Zimmer frame, so that she would have to use a wheelchair. That was, in fact, what eventually happened, even though she was put onto a diet when a new manageress was appointed.

It should be said that the food at the care home was rather good. The menu was varied and there was a choice of dishes. Lunch was the main meal of the day and the residents could choose between three dishes for each of the three courses. On several of my visits a carer would come into my mother's room and tell her what was on the menu that day so that she could make a selection. This usually turned out to be a protracted procedure as, by the time the carer had read out the third item, Mother had forgotten the first two.

Another advantage of the ground floor room was that it was larger than the upstairs one. This meant that, in the last year or so of my mother's life, a mechanical hoist could be used to get her into and out of bed.

At the beginning of March, Anna and I, together with Andrew, Morag and baby Emily, went to see my mother. She seemed to be happy in her new room. Whilst energised by the presence of a baby, she had a lot of difficulty in grasping which of us were the parents. I went again the following week, with a plant and card for Mothering Sunday, and stayed for over an hour. These visits, especially if I was unaccompanied, were monotonous. By this time, Tom and I had reverted to fortnightly visits on alternate weeks, so that she would see one of us each week. Meaningful conversation was impossible owing to the combination of dementia and deafness. From an early stage of Mother living in the care home, I would telephone the home before my visit and ask to see her in her room. Initially this was to avoid the embarrassment of her making comments, often of a derogatory nature, about other residents sitting in the communal lounge. Subsequently, it was to avoid having the following type of conversation, with other residents listening:

"Have you got a girlfriend?"

"No. I'm married to Anna. In fact, I've been married for 37 years."

"I can't remember your wife."

"You would recognise her if you saw her."

"Have you got any children?"

"Yes. I have a daughter, Sarah, and a son, Andrew. They are both married and have a child each of their own. So, I have two granddaughters and you have two great-granddaughters."

And then the same questions would go around in a loop. Occasionally, there would be variations, such as:

"Do you like where you're living?"

"Yes. I've lived there for over 27 years."

"Have I seen your home?"

"Yes, you've stayed there many times."

One of my mother's frequent observations in the communal lounge was that various other residents were asleep in their armchairs. It was not long before she followed their example. It seemed to Tom and me that residents in care homes soon become institutionalised.

She never knew where she was living, despite being told on numerous occasions. She would sometimes point to her bed and ask me whether it was mine, thinking that it was me who was living at the home and that she was visiting.

Tom tended not to ring the home in advance of his visits and, therefore, Mother would quite often have been moved into the lounge before he arrived. He recounted a visit in an email to me in early April.

I went to see Mum yesterday. Whilst she was in very good form, she was completely away with the fairies. In fact, I have never experienced her 'so far gone.' It was quite amusing.

I went in the afternoon and arrived at 3pm. Mum was in the lounge and pleased to see me. At teatime she was under the impression that she was organising everything and wanted to ensure that all the carers offered everyone a cup of tea and piece of cake, as if it were her treat. She wanted to pay for the tea etc. but I assured her that everything was under control and not to worry. She also wanted to make sure that Eileen had a piece of cake. She seemed to think that Eileen was around.

167

> *Mum is still confused about the relationship with her and Dad and wanted to know whether he had married again. At one time she even asked who my mother was. She did, I recall, correct herself...I hope!*
>
> *At one stage in the afternoon, I had to go for a pee and on my return found Mum talking to the pleasant frail old lady who walks with a Zimmer and is bent double. Mum was telling her that she had been busy with the children and was now going shopping. She told her that she would collect her afterwards with a view to going out for dinner.*
>
> *I had a chat with a carer who informed me that Mum had really been confused during the week but was 'quite good today'!!*

When I went to see Mother in mid-April she was in a good mood although, according to the deputy manager, she had been behaving badly. She had been uncooperative on occasions when carers were trying to get her out of bed in the morning to wash and dress her. The more experienced members of staff were generally able to handle her, but the younger ones struggled. She had been very nasty to at least one of the young carers, making personal comments about her appearance and telling her that she wouldn't find a husband. I learned of one amusing ruse employed by a senior carer when my mother was refusing to get out of bed. She was told that she had to hurry because she had to get her boys off to school. That did the trick.

It may have been around that time that Mother frequently talked about her parents, especially her mother, as though they were still alive. Her father had died over 50 years earlier, in his late seventies, and her mother had been dead for nearly 30 years, having lived to her late eighties. She would ask me if I had seen 'Mum' recently and I would simply reply in the negative, not wanting to upset her.

Andrew, Morag and Emily came to stay with us for the May bank holiday weekend and, on the Sunday morning, we went to see Mother. She had no recollection of having seen Emily before and was again very confused as to the relationships between us all. This situation persisted during all subsequent visits made by Emily.

Nothing untoward regarding my mother was recorded in my diary for June and July, albeit that Anna and I were away for much of June.

*

In early August I went to see Eileen. I had prepared a codicil to her will appointing Angela as her executor in place of the nephew who, we had now discovered, was living in Singapore. Whilst I was with her, the codicil was signed and witnessed. Eileen and I also discussed her deposit accounts and how to increase her income. As far as I was aware, it went well. However, I received a telephone call from Angela later that day reporting that Eileen had rung her in a state, very worried about the possibility of removing funds on deposit with her bank. She seemed almost paranoid that she would lose her money if it were moved anywhere else. I subsequently learned that she had rung the bank to say that she did not want any of her money moved.

The building society with which Eileen also had accounts had been acquired by a bank. Eileen had just over £65,000 invested with it in a deposit account and a cash ISA. Both were paying very low rates of interest. A few days after seeing Eileen, I called in at the branch of the bank nearest to my home. With the authority of the power of attorney, I moved the funds into other accounts at the same bank which paid better rates.

*

After leaving the bank, I went to see my mother. She was in an unpleasant mood and clearly depressed. The carer who mostly looked after her told me that her moods were very changeable.

*

The next day I rang Eileen to let her know what I had done with her funds at the second bank and told her she would receive written confirmation from the bank. She said that she recalled that we had discussed those funds but did not seem in the least bit grateful for my efforts. Oh, happy days.

I also attempted to move funds around in Eileen's main bank, but this was not so straightforward. I had done my own banking online for many years and did the same with my mother's. In order to use Internet banking at Eileen's bank, it was first necessary to apply for telephone banking, which I did when I called at my local branch. In anticipation of registering for Internet banking, I opened two new accounts with the bank which paid better rates of interest than the accounts which Eileen then had. However, difficulties arose as soon as I tried to use their online system. I was unable to transfer her funds to the new accounts; neither their Internet helpline nor their telephone banking helpline was able to assist. The only way of effecting the transfers was to make an appointment at the branch.

*

In early September Tom and I went to the annual garden party at my mother's care home. We enjoyed ourselves, which was something we rarely did in those days in our mother's company. She appeared happy as well, albeit in a world of her own as usual, divorced from reality.

*

In mid-September I received a letter from Eileen's bank thanking me for applying for their telephone banking service and asking me to give them a call, in order to complete the registration. I did so on 14th September and, at the same time, registered for online banking too. At least I thought I had. The bank said that I would receive a letter regarding this. I never did.

On a Friday in mid-September Eileen rang me to say that she had bad toothache and wanted to make an appointment with her dentist. She had been advised by the dentist that she ought to have someone with her and, as her carer Pat was unavailable, she wondered if I would accompany her. I agreed to do so. The next morning, she rang again to say that she had now made an appointment for the following Monday. I was rather surprised that she had been able to do this on a Saturday and rang her dentist's surgery on the Monday morning. The receptionist informed me that there was no appointment with my aunt that day. She realised that Eileen had dementia and told me that she telephoned the surgery most days. The receptionist said that she would ask the dentist to call me. I then rang Eileen to let her know that there was no appointment that day. When the dentist called, he told me that he had been unable to find anything wrong with Eileen's teeth and had advised her that the problem appeared to be with her ear.

*

Later that week, Anna and I visited Mother. She was depressed and tearful at first, but we managed to cheer her up. It was always better having Anna there as Mother could hear her better than me. I think it must have been the higher pitch of the female voice. I have a male friend with hearing difficulties, but he finds it easier to hear male voices.

Both our children and their families came to stay with us over the second weekend of October. We all visited the care home on the Saturday. Mother could not grasp which baby belonged to whom.

At the end of October, Tom and I visited Mother together. She was in a happy mood. She was also cheerful when I saw her eight days later. To have something to occupy the time, I showed her photos on my laptop, principally of my house and garden, as she had mentioned on an earlier occasion that she could not remember where I lived. Seeing the photographs did not seem to bring back any memories. It was on such occasions that I felt particularly sorry for her. She had very little quality of life. It is also a lot easier to feel sympathy for someone when they are not being nasty to you.

*

On 16th November, I logged on to Eileen's bank's website and printed out a statement of her various accounts with them. It seemed, however, that I was still not fully registered for online banking as I was unable to transfer funds internally. It was also apparent that Eileen had opened a monthly savings account after the power of attorney had been registered with the bank, and without my knowledge. I therefore rang the bank, pointing out that, despite being informed on 14th September that they would be writing to me regarding Internet banking, they had failed to do so. For reasons too tedious to repeat here, I had to make a further appointment with the branch to sort things out. They arranged for me to see the young woman I had seen three months earlier.

I telephoned Eileen the same day to inform her that better rates of interest than her bank was paying could be obtained at a building society. She said that her bank was now paying 5% on a deposit account. When I expressed doubt about that, she said that she had spoken to the bank and had been advised of that rate. She said she would ring the bank and call me back. When she did so, it transpired that the account was a monthly saver. This was, in fact, the account that she had opened earlier in the year without telling me. I explained to her that it was an account into which you must pay a set amount each month and it did not address the problem of what to do with the large sum in her deposit account on which she was earning very little interest. She said that she had no objection to my moving part of that money to a building society so long as it was not tied up for too long in case she had to go into a care home. That was a revealing comment in that it showed she was aware of that possibility.

*

Tom and I saw our mother together again on 18th November. Mother asked whether we had come to see our sister. One of the senior carers, Jill, was in the room at the time and the three of us thought that Mother was referring to Jill. Later, over lunch, Tom and I wondered if she had been referring to herself as our sister. There were other occasions when she appeared to think I was her brother who, by that time, had been dead for many years.

On this particular joint visit, Mother remembered our names although she appeared uncertain that she was our mother. She also seemed to think that we were just starting out in life. It was particularly poignant when she pointed to the photograph of herself with our father on their wedding day, and asked who the man was.

There were many occasions when my mother was confused as to her own identity. Unless they were specifically recorded in my diary, it is impossible to remember exactly when they occurred, but it was probably about this time that I realised that she no longer remembered what she looked like. She pointed to herself in a couple of family photographs on the wall in her room, taken in 2009, and thought that it was her mother. When I expressed surprise that she did not recognise herself, she replied that she never looked in mirrors. That was clearly wrong as she had a large mirror on a wall in her room, a mirror forming part of her dressing table, and another mirror above the basin in her en-suite lavatory.

*

After seeing my mother on 18th November, I drove to Eileen's bank for the appointment that had been arranged on the telephone. It had been fixed for 2:30. However, when I saw the official I was supposed to meet, she appeared to be unaware of the appointment, asking me with whom I had arranged it. I told her that I had made it through telephone banking and that I had a reference for the appointment. She said that she had been asked by the manager to open a new account for a customer but that she would be able to see me in about 20 minutes. I made it clear that that was not good enough. She then admitted that she did have a note of the appointment, but she had to carry out the job for her manager. She arranged for me to see one of her colleagues.

I explained to the colleague the problems I had been having with online and telephone banking accounts. He showed me notes on his screen to the effect that the customer had retained the ability to operate her accounts, and that Eileen had given instructions that her accounts were not to be removed from her local branch by her attorney. He then tried to transfer online a nominal £1 from one of Eileen's savings accounts to her current account after I accessed the accounts online using my password. Although we were able to see details of her accounts on screen, we were barred from making any transfer. We then tried to clarify the position with telephone banking and online banking but were unable to do so. This involved holding on the phone for a long time on both occasions. Ultimately, I was advised that the solution was to re-register for telephone banking, even though this had been done about three months earlier. I was in the bank for about one and a half hours. Another frustrating experience.

On returning home, I rang the Office of the Public Guardian and was advised that the donor retained the ability to operate her accounts if she had the mental capacity to do so. I asked what I should do in the circumstances as, although my aunt was able to operate her current account, she ought not to be operating her savings accounts. I was advised that the best course of action was to try to come to an arrangement with the bank.

I then rang Eileen's local branch. The telephone was answered by a young woman named Sharon and I asked to speak to a helpful Irish lady with whom I had spoken on earlier occasions. Unfortunately, she was on holiday. I explained the situation to Sharon who said that she had some ideas on the best way of proceeding but needed to speak to a senior person. There was nobody available to speak to me, but she would arrange for her colleague, Louise, to call me the following day.

Sharon rang at lunchtime the next day to tell me that it would be necessary for me to call in at her branch to see one of her colleagues. I explained that, although I was prepared to do so, it was not convenient as it would take me about an hour to get there. She said that I could instead visit my local branch. I told her that I had already done that yesterday to little or no effect. She explained that the bank needed to see the power of attorney and documents proving my identity. As patiently as I could, I pointed out that the power of attorney had been registered with the bank several months ago, and that the bank also had copies of requisite documents demonstrating my identity. I suggested that copies may be available to her on her computer screen. She appeared unable to access the system, so I was left with no alternative but to make a provisional appointment to call at the branch. Before hanging up, I asked what the bank proposed to do about the problem of my aunt's conflicting instructions once I had established yet again that I was her attorney. She offered no opinion but said that Louise would ring me on Monday morning as she had now finished for the day. I protested that Louise was supposed to have rung me today. Sharon said that Louise had asked her to ring. We seemed to be going round in circles.

I telephoned Eileen to inform her of the difficulties I was having with her wretched bank and explained that I suspected that this was partly caused by the instructions she had given them to the effect that her money was to remain in her branch and should not be moved by her attorneys. She denied ever giving such an instruction. She then said that nothing could be done with the savings for six months as she had transferred funds to a six months fixed-term account. I said I knew nothing about this and asked how much had been transferred, when this had taken place and what rate of interest was being paid. She indicated it had happened recently but did not remember the amount, although the interest rate was 5.5%. I expressed incredulity at this, and she said that she would get the letter. She came back to the phone about a minute later and read me a letter dated 9th October which referred to a deposit of £50,000 at a rate of 2%. She commented that this was less than the rate she had been advised over the telephone. I explained that the higher rate she was thinking about was that applicable to the monthly saver account. I then asked her to tell me the date of the letter again and it transpired to have been written over a year ago. I told her that I would be speaking to the bank on Monday and would probably be making an appointment to see them. She agreed to come with me to sort out the problems and confirmed that she had no objection to some of the funds being transferred to a building society.

I next rang Angela to report on the problems I was having and said that if Eileen changed her mind again at the bank, I would resign as her attorney as it was so stressful. Angela said that she did not want to deal with it on her own and would also resign.

The following Tuesday I rang Eileen's branch of the bank to complain that Louise had failed to ring me the previous day, as promised, and had still not rung. Fortunately, the phone was answered by Christine, the personal banker with whom I had spoken early last year and who was aware of Eileen's problems. I explained the difficulties I was having, and she was very helpful. Firstly, she downgraded Eileen's current account, on which she received no interest and took none of the benefits that account offered, to another type on which she would earn interest of 4% per annum on balances up to £7,000. Secondly, Christine explained that I had been unable to transfer funds online from any of Eileen's accounts as a block had been placed on them. This would have been done by the internet banking team, although the reason was not apparent to her. She removed the block. Thirdly, she placed a note on the accounts that no action should be taken on instructions from Eileen regarding her savings accounts without prior reference to me. I expressed my gratitude to Christine. It just took someone to exercise common sense and good judgment to resolve problems that should not have arisen in the first place.

I next rang the building society, to which I wanted to transfer some of Eileen's funds, to check on the procedures for opening an account for a fixed-term bond under a power of attorney. It was confirmed that it could be opened in a branch where I could also register the power of attorney and produce evidence of my identity. However, I could not transfer the funds for the account online. A cheque would be required. I therefore rang Eileen and explained the position to her. She remained amenable to transferring £25,000 but was not prepared to send me a cheque in the post even though I explained that it would be payable to herself. She was so worried about losing the money that she wanted me to collect the cheque from her. The fact that it may have been inconvenient to me did not seem to have occurred to her.

I arranged to see Eileen on 15th December, but she rang to postpone my visit as Pat was going to take her shopping that day.

A major cause for my difficulties in handling Eileen's financial affairs under the lasting power of attorney was that, under the Mental Capacity Act, every adult has the right to make their own decisions and is presumed to have the capacity to do so unless it is proved to the contrary. The situation with my mother was far simpler as her dementia was much worse than Eileen's. Her enduring power of attorney had been registered with the Court of Protection and she was thereafter deemed to be unable to manage her own affairs. With Eileen, on the other hand, it would not have been straightforward to rebut the presumption of capacity. Thus, her bank, when faced with conflicting instructions from Eileen and me, would have had difficulty in deciding what to do. This would particularly have been the case where decisions were taken other than at branch level.

*

On 16th December I went to see my mother, but she was out on a group visit to a local garden centre. Such was her lack of social activities that a visit to a garden centre in December was regarded by the home as a treat. While I was there, I learned that the clothes we were getting her for Christmas had arrived in the post at home. I therefore drove back to the care home in the afternoon with the presents, which were left with the deputy manager, and I saw Mother briefly. She was not in a difficult mood and had not been troublesome during the past few visits.

*

Road conditions had been bad at times that December because of snow. I rang Eileen on 21st December to explain why I had been unable to see her, and I wished her a merry Christmas. She knew that she would not be coming to us as, for the first time in our married life, Anna and I were going to a hotel over the holiday period. This was because neither of our children were coming to stay that year and we did not fancy spending the bulk of Christmas on our own at home.

*

I went to see Mother again on 22nd December and, on that occasion, I stayed for over one and a half hours. A real endurance test, but it made me feel good, even though I knew that after I had gone, she would almost immediately have forgotten I had visited.

Chapter Fourteen

2011

Andrew, Morag and Emily stayed with us over the
New Year weekend. We all went to see Mother on New Year's
Day. She responded well to the baby but had no recollection of
having seen her before.

*

The following day, the five of us went to see Eileen and took
her Christmas presents with us. Whilst there, Eileen gave me a
cheque for £20,000 for the building society investment we had
discussed.

A few days later, I called into my local branch of the
building society with a view to opening the proposed account.
It was apparent that I had insufficient documentary evidence of
Eileen's identity to satisfy their requirements. I therefore made
a further journey to her flat on 12th January where I managed
to find a recent bank statement and an invoice from BT, which
I hoped would suffice. I took these into the building society on

the way home but, after queuing for some time, I was informed that there was nobody available who would be able to help me. I think this was because not all members of staff were competent to handle investments made through a power of attorney. I then called at another building society which was offering the same rate. Unfortunately, the documents I had were insufficient to satisfy their requirements as to proof of Eileen's identity. That afternoon I had a look at the first society's website, and it was apparent that I would have great difficulty in satisfying their conditions regarding her identity as they required to see either a passport or driving licence. Eileen had neither. After a couple of telephone conversations with them, they agreed to accept a recent letter from either HMRC or the Pensions Office. HMRC were unlikely to correspond with my aunt as her tax was deducted at source. I rang Eileen and asked her to look for a letter relating to her State Pension. A little while later she rang me back to say that she did not want to transfer the money out of her bank account. I reminded her that she had already given me a cheque for that purpose, but she was adamant. I rang Angela to let her know what was happening or, rather, not happening. I had wasted the best part of a day in trying to help Eileen. I felt like screaming in frustration.

The following day I wrote the following letter to Eileen:

I refer to your telephone call of early yesterday evening when you indicated that you no longer wished to go ahead with the transfer of £20,000 to a new account to be opened with [the Building Society]. You want the money to remain with [your bank] even though they are paying a very low rate of interest. In the circumstances I am returning the bank statement and the BT invoice you gave me for identification purposes. I have also destroyed your cheque for £20,000 and have transferred that amount from your current account back to your savings account.

The only reason you gave me for not proceeding with this investment was that you would rather your money stayed with [your bank] as you have always banked with them. I feel obliged to point out that this is irrational. Your savings account is earning net annual interest of 1.44% whereas inflation is currently 3.30%. This means that, in real terms, the value of your savings is diminishing. The building society account is paying 2.4% net which, although not exciting, is still significantly more than the bank's rate. Moreover, if I had not transferred your money into the savings account, it would still be in your instant access account which is paying the derisory rate of 0.08%. You might as well have kept your money under the mattress.

You have no idea how much stress and frustration I have suffered in trying to deal with your affairs under a power of attorney, particularly with your bank, or how much time I have spent in trying to earn you a better rate of interest. It has mostly been in vain as you have now, not for the first time, changed your mind at a very late stage regarding an investment.

In the circumstances I feel I can no longer be of help to you.

One final piece of advice. I understood from a recent conversation that you are using your debit card to make payments and that you have a note of the pin number which you keep in your handbag. This is a very dangerous practice and one that banks strongly warn their customers against. If your bag were stolen, the thief would be able to access your current account and your bank might well refuse to reimburse you for the loss suffered. This loss could be substantial in view of the unnecessarily large amount you keep in that account. I think that you should make an appointment with your bank in order to change your pin number to one that you can remember without writing it down.

I am sending a copy of this letter to Angela so that she is aware of the position.

When emailing a copy of that letter to Angela I told her that I would remain Eileen's attorney but would prefer to only become actively involved again in her financial affairs if and when she reached the stage of having to relinquish all control over her finances. Angela replied, expressing sympathy and predicting that Eileen, if true to form, would ring me to say that she did not mean to upset me, and possibly ring Angela to say the same. Eileen did ring 12 days later but, although I recorded in my diary that it was a long conversation, I did not note what was said. As I had no further contact with Eileen for several months, it seems that nothing had changed.

*

A few days later Anna, Andrew, Morag, Emily and I drove to my mother's care home to take birthday cards and presents. We did not see her as we were told that she had only just woken up (it was after 11:00) and was in a very bad mood. This was possibly because she had a chest infection. She had recovered by the time I visited her in early February. Our conversation revealed the wretchedness of her situation. She could not remember the name of her deceased husband. Later she pointed to her wedding photograph and asked whether the woman in the photograph had been happy with him. She did not realise that she was referring to herself. There was a similar occurrence a week later when Tom, Anna and I called to see her. She referred again to the wedding photograph and asked whether the two people in it were still alive.

When I visited her at the end of February, I took my laptop with me so that I could again show her photographs of my house and garden. Although she indicated that some of the views were familiar, I don't think she recognised anything. She also did not appear to recognise my children from their photographs.

I continued to visit my mother at least twice a month but nothing significant happened during this period. She was generally in a good mood. On a visit with Tom in mid-April, however, her mental state was particularly poor. She asked the same questions repeatedly, including whether either of us was married. She could not remember the names of either our wives or our children. She also asked whether the man pictured in two photos on her dressing table was her father. It was her husband. This, to me, demonstrates more vividly than anything the utter tragedy of dementia. Her life was so lacking in quality that she did not even have her memories to cling on to.

*

A few days later, Eileen was taken to the A&E department of her nearest hospital but, when I rang the hospital the following day, it seemed she had recovered from whatever had been wrong with her. The warden at Kingsley Wood only worked weekday mornings but there was an emergency service operating at other times. Eileen got into the habit of ringing them if she did not feel well which was probably more often than was necessary. Their response was generally to call for an ambulance to take her to hospital.

*

Anna and I visited my mother in early May. It was again apparent that she could not remember my father, to whom she had been married for 39 years. This was also another occasion where she appeared to have forgotten what she herself looked like. We went again about two weeks later, this time with Andrew, Morag and Emily, who had come for the weekend.

I next saw Mother at the beginning of June, when she was suffering with another chest infection and feeling miserable. It was possibly about this time when, on arriving at Prince's Manor, I found Mother still in bed and in a truculent mood. My visit was interrupted when a carer came in to dress her. While waiting, I went into the residents' lounge to have a coffee. In there I saw another old lady, named Joan, who I would occasionally chat with. She asked how my mother was, and I remarked that she was being difficult. Joan replied, "Never mind, dear, you're her favourite. She's always saying so." I was very surprised to hear this but quickly realised that Joan was confusing me with Tom. Not content with having a favourite son, my mother had to broadcast it to other people. How much better life would have been if my mother had been a sweet old lady like Joan.

*

Eileen was also feeling unwell that month as she was again taken by ambulance to hospital. I recorded in my diary that I had telephone conversations with both the hospital and Angela on 13th June regarding Eileen. As there were no other calls noted during the following four days, I presume that she was merely seen in A&E and then sent home. There was then a flurry of activity.

On the afternoon of Saturday, 18th June, I received several telephone calls from Eileen's emergency service. It appears that Eileen rang them to say that she had a hospital appointment that day, but her carer had not turned up to take her. I explained to the young woman who rang that it was highly unlikely that Eileen had an appointment on a Saturday and that the carer would probably not be working on a Saturday in any event. I gave her the carer's number, but she was unable to speak to anyone. Eileen also said that she could barely walk and was unable to care for herself. During a subsequent call, it was apparent that Eileen had recovered the ability to walk. The young woman said that Eileen was clearly confused and that she too was getting confused. She eventually called the ambulance service who could decide if Eileen needed to be admitted to hospital. She later reported to me that the service had taken the view that my aunt did not need to be admitted but that they would arrange for a doctor to visit her.

I rang Eileen on 20th June to find out how she was. She said that she was not at all good and was finding it difficult to know what to eat as she was having problems with her bowels. She was due to have a colonoscopy carried out. She seemed surprised to learn that the emergency service had spoken to me on Saturday. She agreed that she did not have a hospital appointment that day but did say that Pat had not been for ages. She was, however, waiting for a lady from 'welfare' to call to see her. This had apparently been arranged by Age Concern to whom Eileen had spoken. I said that I would contact Social Services to try to speak to Pat.

Fortunately, I was able to contact Pat who informed me that she saw Eileen every week and had been as recently as last Friday. It appeared that she had discussed with Eileen the desirability of appointing a care agency so that she received daily visits from a carer. As Eileen's savings exceeded £23,250, she would have to meet the cost of the services herself. I was fully in agreement with the proposals. Pat also said that she thought it would do Eileen a lot of good to visit a day centre where she would be able to chat with other elderly people and would get a hot meal every day. Eileen had not been in favour of this.

Pat was helpful and sensible. She was well aware of Eileen's hypochondria and tendency to cry wolf. She mentioned a recent occasion when Eileen had rung in an apparent emergency and Pat had rushed round to see her, only to discover that there was nothing wrong and Eileen chatted away happily. She also said that Eileen tended to look to various people for help which could cause problems. I warned Pat, in this connection, that Eileen had apparently been in touch with Age Concern over the weekend. Pat said that she would go and see Eileen that day. In the course of our conversation, she mentioned that Eileen's colonoscopy was due to be carried out early next month and she would be taking Eileen to the hospital.

I rang Eileen to inform her of my conversation with Pat. She initially denied saying that Pat had not been to see her for ages but, a few minutes later, she repeated the allegation.

It was interesting that Eileen, just like my mother, had no interest in going to a day centre. I think their reasons may have been different. Both were socially isolated, and it would probably have benefited them to attend. My mother's reluctance was possibly due to a belief that it was beneath her, Eileen's to her timidity.

I received a telephone call a few days later from the care agency appointed by Pat to look after Eileen. They told me that Pat had been through the contract terms with her to ensure that she understood what she was signing. Eileen had also completed a direct debit mandate. The arrangement was for a carer to call in for 15 minutes in the morning, 30 minutes at lunchtime and 15 minutes in the evening. These coincided with the times that Eileen took her medication about which, apparently, she had been getting confused. I was told that, as Eileen had enjoyed the Tesco frozen meals that Pat got her, a carer would microwave one of these at the lunchtime visit. If it transpired that Eileen preferred her main meal in the evening, the agency would change their arrangements so that the 30-minute visit was made then. According to my calculations, the cost of the care service would be £168 a week.

I reported all of this to Angela and expressed concern that we might be at the stage where we needed to take over the management of Eileen's financial affairs. That was something that I would try to discuss with Pat on my return from a forthcoming holiday.

Whilst I was away, Angela telephoned Eileen to enquire as to her health and was amazed by the change in her. She was happy and laughing and, most unusually, did not mention her ailments. She was delighted with the carers calling in three times a day and said how nice they were. She was also enjoying the food they were preparing. Although Angela knew the answer, she asked Eileen whether she had to pay for the carers, but Eileen did not know; she said, however, that she would be more than happy to pay as it was worth it. It seemed that she did not recall signing the contract or the direct debit form. The care arrangement was clearly a success, albeit rather expensive.

I managed to speak to Pat on 20th July. She had taken Eileen to her appointment with the consultant. It appeared that Eileen had recovered from the complaint from which she had been suffering. Pat indicated, however, that Eileen's mental health was deteriorating and that she was very confused at times.

This accorded with my own view and I decided, with Angela's agreement, to take control of Eileen's finances, albeit in a way that would minimise any anxiety she might feel. In this regard after numerous unsuccessful attempts over several days to contact the branch of her bank, where she kept her account, the phone was eventually answered. I arranged that the bank would not allow Eileen to set up any further direct debits without obtaining my prior approval or, if I was unavailable, Angela's.

I also went through Eileen's various bank accounts online. This revealed that she had, excluding investments in funds operated by a subsidiary, just under £69,000 with the bank, the great majority of which was in accounts that were paying a very low rate of interest. Where applicable I considered alternative investments which I discussed with Angela. Of even more concern, however, was the fact that substantial sums were being withdrawn from Eileen's current account via a cash point. For the period from 6th May to 15th July, there were the following withdrawals:

> 6th May £200
> 6th May £100
> 17th May £300
> 3rd June £300
> 1st July £100
> 1st July £100
> 15th July £300

Neither Angela nor I could understand why Eileen would have the need for so much cash: she paid for almost everything by direct debit, apart from her supermarket shopping for which she paid by debit card.

A few days later I spoke to Pat. She confirmed that Eileen did withdraw cash on occasions when Pat took her shopping, although she seemed surprised by the sums I mentioned. She suggested that Eileen might have hidden cash at home and then either forgotten that she had it or forgotten where it was hidden. Pat said that she had come across this problem before with old people. That seemed plausible to me as, when I had been sorting out Eileen's papers a few years earlier, I had come across quite a lot of cash in an envelope that she had forgotten she had.

In early August I went to see Eileen. She was unable to throw any light on why so much cash had been withdrawn. We discussed her financial matters generally and she was happy to write a cheque for £20,000 so that I could invest the money elsewhere at a higher rate of interest. I also removed a lot of papers to take home so that I could sort them out and put them into a sensible filing system. She had not been using the concertina file that I had set up for her a couple of years earlier. Just as my mother had done, Eileen had simply stuffed papers, regardless of their subject matter or chronology, into drawers in different items of furniture.

On the same day, I contacted Pat and asked her to restrict Eileen to withdrawing no more than £50 a fortnight. Both Angela and I suspected that Pat may have been stealing the cash. However, although I had not met her, I had spoken to her over the telephone on several occasions and she seemed to be a sensible and conscientious person. In any event, if she was involved, she would know that I was now keeping a careful eye on the withdrawals.

At some stage, and I cannot remember why, a decision was taken for Eileen to have her lunch delivered by Meals on Wheels.

I was continuing to visit my mother every couple of weeks, but there were no problems with her at that time. This was fortunate as I was so busy with Eileen's affairs. I sorted out Eileen's papers, threw away a lot of them, and arranged the rest into various categories; invested her £20,000 in a building society bond that was paying 3.5% per annum; in conjunction with Pat, applied for Attendance Allowance; cut out the care agency's lunchtime visit when the Meals on Wheels service commenced; and applied to register with the Office of the Public Guardian the power of attorney relating to Eileen's health and welfare. This was a matter I had mentioned to Eileen on my recent visit and she was clearly unenthusiastic about it, fearing that she might be sent to a care home. I nevertheless felt it was essential to proceed considering her deteriorating mental health. To avoid causing her distress, I paid the registration fee of £120 out of my own pocket, although I recouped it later.

On 17th August I received an email from Angela reporting on a telephone call she had received from a lady named Tina from Eileen's bank. Eileen had rung them a couple of times to say that £20,000 was missing from her account and she thought that I was using the power of attorney to steal from her. Angela had explained that the money had, with Eileen's agreement, been invested elsewhere but that Eileen must have forgotten. Tina said she had presumed that that was the case as a similar complaint had been made before. Whilst I appreciated that Eileen was suffering from dementia, it was nevertheless distressing that she should accuse me of dishonesty, particularly in view of all the work I had been doing on her behalf. If nothing else, it made me realise how sensible it had been to insist that Angela should be appointed as a joint attorney, and to have kept her informed of everything that I was doing. At least she was supportive and sympathetic, as was June, my other aunt, whom Angela kept informed. It was ironic that Eileen should accuse me of theft but be unable to offer any explanation for the cash withdrawals from her current account.

I finished going through Eileen's papers, but they were incomplete. So, on 18th August, I faxed Tina with various queries and requests. One of these was to ask if it was possible to stop representatives of the bank from telephoning my aunt to sell products such as savings accounts or insurance policies. An example of this was an insurance policy to protect against identity theft. As Eileen did not own a PC, and was wholly unfamiliar with the Internet, this policy was quite unnecessary, but presumably earned the bank commission. Indeed, I discovered that she had been persuaded to take out two similar policies on separate occasions. I was able to cancel the direct debits.

In common with other clearing banks, Eileen's bank had some years earlier introduced a system whereby a customer who wished to telephone the bank had to ring a call centre. It was sadly apparent from Eileen's correspondence that this system caused her a huge amount of difficulty. There were letters from the bank, going back several years, which were written following calls she had made, but in which she had been unable to identify herself because she had forgotten her security number. They would send her another number, but she would forget that too. Her confusion became so bad that, by August 2011, there were several letters a week from the bank in the standard form. Telephone banking is simply not appropriate for old people suffering from memory problems.

As well as writing to the bank on 18th August, I also wrote to Eileen to confirm that I had transferred £20,000 from a savings account to her current account so that there would be sufficient funds to meet the cheque that she had given me for investment. I also asked her whether I could cancel her credit card as she did not seem to be using it apart from paying for a subscription to a magazine, several issues of which were in her flat, still in their wrappers. I made no reference to her accusation.

Eileen's response to my letter is reported in an email I sent to Angela a few days later.

Eileen rang me on Friday with regard to my letter. She indicated that she did not want me to cancel her credit card. After some discussion, it became apparent that she thought I was talking about her debit card. I am therefore proceeding as planned. She said she wished to keep her magazine subscription. This is a little difficult as she pays by monthly debit to her credit card. I will contact the publishers and try to change to either a standing order or direct debit to her bank account.

At no time in the conversation did Eileen thank me for any of the work I have done on her behalf. To make matters worse, when Tina from [the bank] rang me the next day with regard to my fax, she said that a message had been received from Eileen wanting to cancel the power of attorney as she had had a falling out with her nephew. This is simply not true. I will continue to manage her affairs but want as little contact with her as possible. Apart from feeling thoroughly fed up, I fear there is a risk that people might begin to believe I am defrauding her. I am afraid that I will have to leave it to you to communicate with her in so far as that is necessary. I will return her bank statements plus the papers I no longer need (keeping everything else here) and that is as far as I intend to go as far as voluntary contact is concerned. Incidentally, I think she will react badly when she receives notification of the application to register the second power of attorney. I did, of course, discuss this with her but it is unlikely she will remember that.

It was, of course, wishful thinking that I would be able to avoid direct contact with Eileen.

One of the difficulties of operating under a power of attorney is the way in which some organisations apply the Data Protection Act. I spoke to the publishers of the magazine to which Eileen subscribed, explaining that I had recently cancelled my aunt's credit card, which she used to pay her monthly subscription, and asked them to send me a direct debit form for completion so that I could switch payment to her current account. They informed me that they were prohibited from doing so by the Data Protection Act as the form would contain my aunt's membership number. They asked me to write to them explaining the position so that they could consider it further. I accordingly did so. I also explained that I could not send them a copy of the power of attorney at that time as the original was with the Pensions Office. I did, however, send them a copy of a letter from the Office of the Public Guardian confirming registration of the power. They did not bother to reply.

At the end of August, Eileen left two very unpleasant telephone messages for Angela in which she claimed that I was trying to kill her with stress in order to get her money and that, if she did not hear from Angela, she would assume that she was in league with me. She considered that our behaviour was despicable. When Angela rang her back, Eileen denied making any such accusation or, indeed, that she had alleged fraud against me to her bank. Angela told me that it was impossible to reason with Eileen and that she was like a child who had been caught out and was insisting that they were innocent.

I find it very sad that her dementia caused Eileen to distrust the two members of her family who were actively trying to help her. The strange thing was that whenever I saw her to discuss her investments, she seemed to understand the advice I gave her and accept it. Subsequently, left on her own, a type of paranoia seemed to set in. Although she made accusations about me behind my back, she was never unpleasant to my face. Indeed, she was generally cheerful, and we nearly always got on well.

*

Andrew, Morag and Emily came to stay with us for the weekend at the beginning of September. On the Saturday I went with them to see my mother. She seemed happy.

*

In the morning of 5th September, I went to see Eileen to return her file of bank statements and various other papers I no longer needed. I rang her beforehand to make sure she was not going to be out shopping with Pat. Eileen told me that she had lost her debit card. I explained that it was important to ring the bank immediately to notify them and to request a new card. I offered to do so but she insisted on doing it herself. When I arrived, it was apparent that she had not contacted the bank. This was even though, when I asked her whether she had cash available, she had only been able to produce one £10 note. She was more concerned with having received several letters from her bank, of the type to which I have referred earlier, saying that someone had rung but they had been unable to identify the person to whom they were speaking. Eileen thought that someone had been pretending to be her. I tried to explain to her that it was almost certainly her who had rung the bank but had been unable to recall her identification number. She did not, needless to say, remember making the calls. When I was there I let her know that I was very upset to learn that she had been accusing me of fraud. As could be anticipated, she denied having made any accusations.

When I got home I contacted Eileen's bank about her debit card and ordered a replacement. It was agreed that she would retain the existing pin number as there was little hope of her remembering a new one. I also mentioned to the bank that I had seen from my aunt's most recent bank statement that three purchases had been made from Tesco within a three-week period and for relatively large amounts. They were able to inform me that all three purchases had been made from Eileen's nearest store and each had included a £50 cashback payment. This worried me as I had specifically instructed Pat that she should not allow Eileen to withdraw more than £50 in cash a fortnight. I did not know, of course, whether Eileen herself had received all or any of that cash. I expressed my concerns to the bank and the lady to whom I spoke suggested that either I should change the carer or give her the card and make her responsible for accounting for the expenditure. She also mentioned that there were notes on the account records that Eileen had rung on several occasions to say that I was defrauding her. Fortunately, the bank staff knew better.

Following my call to the bank, I rang Eileen and asked her whether she had requested cashback on her visits to Tesco. She said that she had not done so for a long time. Although Eileen was a wholly unreliable witness, I now had real cause for concern over Pat's honesty. I knew that Eileen sometimes ordered her groceries from Sainsbury's over the telephone and I asked her to ensure that she only bought groceries in that way in the future. I also advised her that she should never let Pat have her card. It was unlikely she would remember.

Anna and I discussed what to do. We were reluctant to try to get Pat replaced as that could amount to an implication of dishonesty and she might have been entirely innocent. Moreover, she had been helpful in other respects. We came up with a course of action for which I obtained Angela's agreement when I brought her up to date with the day's events. What I did was to write to Pat, after first telephoning her, to say that I was concerned about the amount Eileen appeared to be spending at Tesco. To enable me to monitor her expenditure, I requested her to send me, at the end of each month, the detailed till receipts she obtained from whichever supermarkets she visited with Eileen. I enclosed some stamped-addressed envelopes for that purpose. I also asked her, once again, to ensure that Eileen did not withdraw cash of more than £50 per fortnight but, this time, I referred to cashback as well as a cashpoint.

Anna and I had a week away in mid-September with Andrew, Morag and Emily. On my return, I went to see my mother and was pleased to find her in a happy mood. Unfortunately, later that day, further problems arose with Eileen. These are recorded in an email that I sent to Angela.

I had a call yesterday from Jo, a colleague of Pat, who will be dealing with Eileen during Pat's holiday. She said that she will be going to see Eileen on Thursday (tomorrow) to take her shopping but, before doing so, she wanted to ensure either that Eileen had available cash or could remember her pin number. Jo had accompanied Pat last week when they called on Eileen. The latter did not want to go shopping with them and could not recall her pin number. I said that I understood that Eileen kept a note of her pin number in her handbag. Jo then indicated that the number is written down in a notebook that is kept in the bag. This book was given to Pat plus the debit card and £20 in cash, just in case. It appears that there were several pin numbers noted in the book and Pat was unable to remember the correct one. She tried two, but they were incorrect, so she used the cash. When speaking to Eileen recently, I had specifically told her never to give her pin number to Pat or anyone else.

Jo repeated a point that Pat had already made to me. The carer is only supposed to accompany the person shopping and not to do the shopping for them. Eileen has, apparently, increasingly been reluctant to go with them. It appears that they are not happy about this. I asked Jo to explain this to Eileen again tomorrow and that, if there was a problem, she should ring me.

Following the conversation, I rang Eileen to ask if she could remember her pin number. She could not. I explained that she would have to get a new number and that I would telephone the bank. She, however, insisted on doing so. I asked her to call me back in 15 minutes, but she did not do so. I then rang her again and she was rather vague about whether or not she had rung the bank, but it appeared that she had done so. I telephoned them to check the position. This call took 30 minutes. I eventually discovered that there had been two earlier calls. In the second one, Eileen had been confused and they had thought she needed a new identity number for telephone banking purposes. This is being sent to her. She had not asked the bank for a new pin number and so I did so.

I rang Eileen back and tried to explain the position to her, but I don't think much got through. I will ring her on Friday to see if she has got the new pin number and will try to get it from her so that, if a similar problem occurs in the future, at least I might be able to assist.

Eileen indicated that she had at least £20 in cash, and I informed Jo of this when I rang her back this morning. I suggested that it might be necessary to take

Eileen into her nearest branch so that she can cash a cheque.

I got the impression from speaking with Eileen that she did not appreciate the significance of a pin number and that this was all a fuss about little or nothing.

Three days later, there were more problems. Meals on Wheels rang me to say that their service was simply not working for Eileen. She was ringing them almost daily, sometimes more than once, to cancel delivery. The lady who contacted me said she had visited my aunt twice and was able to confirm that she had not eaten the food that had been left for her. She said that Eileen had visibly lost weight between the two visits. When I called Eileen, she was very confused and was unable to make a decision regarding future meals. In the circumstances I cancelled the Meals on Wheels service and arranged for the care agency to resume lunchtime visits. They agreed to make 45-minute visits, serve a pre-prepared meal, and sit with Eileen to try to ensure that she ate it. In addition, I arranged for the agency's cleaner to go through Eileen's freezer and to throw away any food that was past its use-by date.

In addition to her mental problems, Eileen had also been diagnosed with ulcerated colitis and diverticulitis. In early October it was apparent that her colitis was causing her problems. She was frequently contacting Pat or Brenda, the warden of the sheltered accommodation, to complain of stomach pain or rectal bleeding. She was also ringing the helpline for the out-of-hours care service requesting an ambulance. They had a note on their records to telephone me every time they received a distress call from her. I do not know the origin of that procedure, but it did not emanate from me. I received one of these calls at 5:20 am on Saturday, 8th October, to report that Eileen had called to say that she was haemorrhaging and requested an ambulance. The care service decided not to comply with the request on that occasion but did so later when Eileen rang again that morning. She was taken to hospital and kept under observation. From what I had gathered from earlier conversations with Pat and Brenda, Eileen occasionally bled when having a bowel movement, but this could not properly be described as a haemorrhage. The general view was that, although colitis can be painful and unpleasant, it was something that she had to learn to live with and could be alleviated by having a suitable diet. I suspected that her confusion was causing her hypochondria to run riot.

There had been little variety in Eileen's diet for many years. It seemed from talking to her, and from what I saw in her kitchen, that her main meal comprised either a baked potato or a piece of fish. Such fruit as she ate appeared to be mainly tinned rather than fresh. It was as if she had not really moved on from the war years. Now that she was eating frozen meals prepared by the carers, her diet was more varied, but she was eating very little.

Both Angela and I thought that Eileen was close to the stage where she needed to move to a residential care home. I carried out a review of Eileen's financial position to see if she had the necessary funds to move into a private care home. Although the cost would have exceeded her income by almost £35,000 a year, I calculated that she had sufficient capital invested to cover at least five years' fees before having to use the proceeds of sale of her flat. The figures would need to be revised if she had to go into a nursing home where the fees would have been considerably higher. Angela and I agreed, however, that it would be desirable for Eileen to remain in her sheltered accommodation for as long as possible, with additional home care, as she seemed happy there.

Eileen remained in the hospital for 16 days or so; for almost the entirety of that time she was in the Medical Assessment Unit. During that period, I telephoned on several occasions to enquire about her health and, on 14th October, I went to visit her. I learned that the tests she had undergone had not indicated anything new. She had been given a course of antibiotics and steroids. It was not clear to me what had caused the rectal bleeding. Her main problem seemed to be that she was eating very little and was frail.

*

During this period Anna and I went to visit my mother. She was going through a reasonably trouble-free spell, thank goodness.

*

I arranged with the care agency for a carer to visit Eileen, once she was back home, for 30 minutes in the morning and 15 minutes in the early evening, as well as the 45-minute lunchtime session. I asked them to keep a running shopping list and ring me periodically to let me know what was needed. Pat had contacted a company that produced meals that could be cooked from frozen. She knew of a couple of old ladies at Kingsley Wood who had these meals. She got hold of a few brochures and gave one to Eileen as well as sending me one. This would enable Eileen to choose her meals in advance, which I could then order for her.

Pat arranged with the hospital that she would collect Eileen at 2:00 pm on the day of her discharge. She telephoned on two occasions to confirm this. When she arrived, however, my aunt's medications were not available, and they had to be delivered later to her flat. Pat was surprised at Eileen's physical state. She was frailer than she had been prior to her admission, was very confused and could barely walk. Pat did not think Eileen was in a fit state to have been discharged. Moreover, although Eileen had received dietary advice when in hospital, no dietary sheet was provided on her discharge.

I went to see Eileen on the day after her discharge from hospital. When I arrived, she was dressed and sitting in her armchair. Although she was not as confused as I had anticipated, her physical state was such that I agreed that she should have remained in hospital. She was complaining that the carer had left on the kitchen lights and she seemed unable to get up to turn them off. I did so for her and made her a coffee. Her ankles were swollen; she also said that she was troubled by her osteoporosis. She later got up to go to the lavatory and was having to support herself by holding on to items of furniture. I rang Pat to ask her to try to get hold of a Zimmer frame on a short-term basis. Pat told me that she had done a little shopping for Eileen and had had to use some of her own cash as Eileen had hardly any left. I was unable to find any in the flat but did, however, find a load of post in her bedroom, including bank statements, of which I had previously been unaware, and took a lot of them home. I gave Eileen cash of £60 in exchange for a cheque.

I reported to Angela on Eileen's situation. She informed me that June had rung Eileen who, apparently, did not know why she had been in hospital. Angela thought it was a good sign, however, that Eileen was back to complaining about her osteoporosis, as that indicated that she was no longer so concerned about her other problems.

*

The following day, 26th October, I had an appointment regarding an investment bond of my mother's that was about to mature. After that I went to visit her. She seemed reasonably happy.

*

Shortly before I left Mother, I received a call from Anna who had heard from Brenda. Eileen had come down to her office, shivering with cold. Her central heating was not working and nor was her electric heater. Moreover, Brenda had had to let Eileen's carer in both yesterday and that morning as Eileen was still in bed when the carer arrived. The carers did not have a key to the flat, only to the outside door of the building. Brenda had managed to fix the heater. It appeared that a fuse had blown. She could not, however, get the central heating to work. She informed Anna that it was only Eileen and Beryl who had gas boilers. The other flats were all-electric.

Anna and I drove over to Kingsley Wood as soon as I got home. We could not work out how to fix the boiler and, unfortunately, there was no instruction manual. It was apparent that there could not be much wrong with it as the hot water side of it was working. Anyway, I rang British Gas, with whom there was a maintenance agreement, and arranged for an engineer to call the following morning. Eileen did not seem to have a second key to her flat, so Anna and I went to get some more cut. I put one in the key safe, left one in the flat, and brought one home. Eileen remained very confused. When we initially got to her, we asked her whether the carer had been to make her lunch and she said that she had. A few minutes later, the carer arrived.

Whilst there I took the opportunity to bring home the rest of the papers I had found on my previous visit.

The next day Brenda called me to say that the British Gas engineer had fixed the central heating. To our mutual embarrassment, it was simply a matter of the thermostat having been turned down to zero. I admitted that I had not noticed any thermostat in the flat. Possibly Eileen had turned it down and then forgotten she had done so. Brenda also told me that the carer had been a little late that morning, and Eileen had been on the phone three times to the out-of-hours call centre complaining about this. The call centre had no connection whatsoever with the company providing the carers.

Although Eileen appeared to have thrown away very little in the way of papers over the years, I had difficulty in finding all relevant documentation relating to the substantial investments she had made in her bank's investment company subsidiary. I had been in correspondence with the latter, attempting to obtain additional information, but they were making me jump through hoops to satisfy their interpretation of the money laundering regulations. For example, they required me to provide documentary evidence of Eileen's name and address even though she had been living at her current address when the investments had been taken out, they had always written to her at that address, and they had seen an official copy of the power of attorney bearing her name, address and signature. Even after all that, they would not correspond directly with me but insisted in addressing their correspondence to Eileen, albeit to my address. They also insisted in sending a copy to her own address. I was worried that this would reawaken her paranoia that I was defrauding her.

I had been aware for some time that Eileen had a safety deposit box at her bank and was therefore surprised, when ploughing through her papers, to come across the original lease of her flat. That was something that should have been kept securely, so I made an appointment with the bank in order to place it in the box and, at the same time, find out what treasures it contained.

I also came across a potentially serious problem in Eileen's papers relating to her gas account. She had had a letter from her gas supplier stating that a recent reading was far higher than the norm and requesting her to take a meter reading. I did this when I was there on 25th October and subsequently spoke to the supplier. My reading was consistent with theirs. If correct, it meant that Eileen could have had arrears of well in excess of £2,000. It was possibly a false alarm as I had seen from the correspondence that a similar letter had been received about a year earlier, but the usual monthly deductions were not increased. There was, presumably, some further correspondence but, if so, I had not come across it. I could understand how difficulties may have arisen. Eileen's meter was in an external box next to Beryl's meter box and neither was identified with the flat number. I thought I had got it right as I had traced the pipe leading from Eileen's flat to the meter I read. Anyway, the supplier said it would have a further reading carried out and would also check the relevant meter numbers. In the worst-case scenario, Eileen's monthly payments would increase considerably to clear the balance.

By this time, I had run up quite a lot of expenditure on Eileen's behalf and thought it was now appropriate to obtain reimbursement. I discussed this with Angela who had no objection. I produced an itemised list of expenses, for which I had kept receipts (which is very important when acting under a power of attorney, in case your expenditure is challenged), and emailed it to her for approval. To be on the safe side, I also informed Eileen's bank of what I was proposing to do. While speaking to the bank, I mentioned that I had seen that Eileen's credit card had not been cancelled in accordance with my instruction. It was explained that this could not be done because of the direct debit in respect of the magazine subscription. This problem was easily solved. In view of the publisher's dogmatic attitude in respect of its interpretation of the Data Protection Act, I simply cancelled the subscription.

Eileen would not miss the magazine. She was no longer reading it.

*

On 10th November I went to see my mother. Initially, she thought I was either her husband or a boyfriend. Tom had told me that she sometimes treated him as if he were a suitor. It was difficult enough visiting my demented 87-year-old mother without her flirting with me. Still, at least she was in a good mood.

*

On 14th November I telephoned Pat who said that Eileen had been in a 'whingey mood' during a recent visit. She had not wanted to go through the frozen meals brochure. Pat had observed that Eileen had run out of toilet paper and was using kitchen towels in the bathroom. Pat had therefore added toilet paper to the shopping list made by the care agency. There was only one other item on it. Eileen was apparently only picking at her food, and the contents of the freezer did not appear to have gone down by much since Pat's last visit. Pat had looked at the carers' attendance book and had seen a reference to Eileen having said, on one occasion, that she did not want anything to eat, and on another that she had already eaten. Eileen's electric kettle was not working properly, so Brenda had had to lend her one.

After speaking to Pat, I rang the care agency. I asked that it be reiterated to the carers that, whilst I appreciated that they could not force-feed Eileen, they should cook her a meal whether she wanted it or not, and then stay to see if she ate any of it. I also mentioned that I had not had a telephone call regarding shopping needs since the system was put into operation. This was apparently due to a breakdown in communication at the agency. It seemed sometimes that I was battling incompetence on all sides.

I looked through the frozen meals brochure and placed an order for five mini meals to be delivered to Eileen's flat. I learned that they also delivered to Eileen's neighbour, Beryl, who had recently returned to her flat after a lengthy spell in hospital. I was impressed by the variety of dishes in the brochure and, based on the photographs, their appearance. I thought Eileen would enjoy the food.

I had two telephone conversations with the care agency the following day. In the first, they informed me that one of their care workers was cleaning Eileen's flat, but that Eileen was complaining of feeling ill and had asked the carer not to use the vacuum. The carer was continuing to clean, but clearly was unable to do it properly. In mid-afternoon they reported that Eileen had been feeling unwell, and apparently had had very little to eat or drink over the past couple of days. The carer had called for an ambulance and, on arrival, the ambulance men had tested Eileen and had found that her blood sugar levels were low. They had taken her to hospital for further tests. It was agreed that home visits by the carers would be put on hold pending Eileen's return.

I rang the hospital shortly before 6:00 pm and learned that Eileen was in A&E but had not yet been seen by a doctor. I explained that it was very important that I was informed of when she was due to be discharged as I would have to arrange for her carers to recommence home visits. I was assured that, as I was shown in Eileen's notes as her next-of-kin, I would be informed.

The next day, 16th November, I went to Eileen's bank to look through the contents of her safety deposit box, and to put her lease in it. As I had anticipated, it contained nothing to set the pulse racing. There were 20 share certificates, most of which were obsolete. While I was out, I bought an electric kettle and then delivered it to Eileen's flat. Shortly after arriving I answered her telephone. It was the hospital calling me, which I found strange, as they knew that Eileen lived alone. They informed me that she had a bladder infection but could be discharged. Unfortunately, they had a transport shortage and therefore wanted me to collect her after lunch. I explained that this was inconvenient as I did not live nearby. I was told that the only alternative was to send Eileen home in a taxi. As I did not want her being moved in that manner, especially as she lived on the first floor, I agreed to collect her between 2:30 and 3:00 pm. So, I drove home, had lunch and then drove to the hospital with Anna. We arrived shortly before 3:00 but were kept hanging around for about an hour because the medication was not available. We then took her home and settled her in. She seemed quite perky, although looked very frail. I had arranged earlier for the carers to resume their duties that evening, and I updated Angela on developments. Indeed, I was updating Angela on almost a daily basis.

On 1st December, Eileen was taken to hospital by ambulance at lunchtime. She rang the helpline just before the carer arrived. The message I received from the care agency was that the ambulancemen had said that her blood sugar levels were low because she was not eating properly. She was discharged the next day. I collected her in the afternoon and drove her home. I was again kept waiting for quite a long time at the hospital. Eileen was befuddled, although the fact that she had been discharged so quickly suggested that the hospital could not find much wrong with her. I had earlier heard from the care agency with a very small shopping list, and I took the items with me when I collected her. Whilst with her, I suggested that she might now be better off in a residential care home, and that she might like to have a look at where my mother lived. She did not seem averse to the idea.

I informed Angela of my conversation with Eileen regarding the care home. She telephoned Eileen on Sunday, 4th December, to see if she remembered any of it. The phone rang for some time before Eileen answered and it seemed to Angela that, unfortunately, she had got Eileen out of bed, even though it had gone noon. She said Eileen's speech was slurred and Eileen had no desire to talk, which indicated to Angela that she was in a bad state as she would normally talk non-stop. Eileen said she felt unwell and was aching all over. Angela told her to go back to bed, which Eileen appeared very eager to do. She did not seem to know if the carer was coming.

The following day I spoke to Pat. She agreed that Eileen would be better off in a care home, as all she now did was sit in her armchair hugging a hot water bottle. She was oblivious to what was going on around her. She commented that Eileen's deterioration over the past few months was obvious. She was about to visit her and would check to see whether she had eaten anything that day.

I next rang the manager of Prince's Manor and spoke to her about Eileen, including her colitis, dementia and not eating. She confirmed that they had a couple of vacancies and suggested that I should bring Eileen in to have a look at the place. If she found it to her liking, Eileen could come and stay for a couple of weeks over Christmas to see how she got on. She could be assessed during that period to see if she was suitable for the home.

I called Eileen. She took a long time to answer the telephone and appeared to have little or no recollection of our conversation regarding the care home. She initially said she did not want to go in that week as she was not feeling well. I observed that she had not been feeling well for several months which was why I felt she should be in a care home, where she would be looked after. I stressed that, at this stage, it was merely being proposed that she should go and have a look at the place to see whether she liked it. After some persuasion on my part, she agreed to come with me on Wednesday of that week, and that I would collect her at 10:00 am. She wrote this down.

I then telephoned the manager of Prince's Manor and made an appointment. I also rang the care agency to say that it was essential that Eileen was up, dressed and ready to leave by 10:00 on Wednesday.

On Tuesday Pat rang me to report on her visit to Eileen the previous day. She said that, when she arrived, Eileen was very feeble, but she soon perked up and became chatty. Pat kindly agreed to be at the flat at 9:00 the next day to make sure that Eileen was ready to leave on time.

Early the next day, I received telephone calls from the carer and Pat to say that Eileen was very poorly and was refusing to get up. I cancelled the appointment at the care home. I did, however, go there on my own to see my mother and took the opportunity of having a further talk with the manager about Eileen. She remained prepared to take her in for a trial period to include Christmas.

Three days later, 10th December, Eileen was back in hospital, apparently with another urinary tract infection. Initially she was in the Medical Assessment Unit and I experienced a considerable amount of frustration in trying to find anyone to speak to on the telephone; either the phone was not answered, or people were unavailable or did not return calls. I was becoming somewhat anxious: the care home had been keeping a room available since

7th December and I wanted to ensure the manager was updated so that we could move Eileen there as soon as she was discharged. Eventually, I managed to speak to a helpful staff nurse. It seemed that Eileen would be discharged within a few days.

On 13th December, I drove to Eileen's flat and, with help from Brenda, packed a suitcase with clothes and filled two cardboard boxes with other stuff, all of which was to go to the care home. While there, I tidied up the flat, as it was in a deplorable state. It looked as if the care agency's cleaner had not been for a long time, probably because of Eileen's frequent visits to hospital. I also took home more paperwork that might need attention. That afternoon I was informed by a junior doctor at the hospital that Eileen would be discharged on 15th December. She agreed to telephone me that morning to let me know if Eileen was well enough to be collected. I was due to go on a walk with a friend that day, but I cancelled it.

15th December arrived, but the doctor failed to call. On ringing the hospital, I learned that Eileen had been moved to another ward. After several further calls it was established that she was too ill to leave before Monday, 19th December at the earliest. That afternoon I drove to the hospital to take Eileen some clothes and toiletries. She was asleep when I arrived, and I did not disturb her.

On 19th December I learned from the hospital that the doctor considered that my aunt was medically fit to be discharged, but she would need to be assessed to see if she was physically fit enough. On several occasions during her time in hospital, I was informed about problems with her legs. This information varied according to the day or the person to whom I was speaking. Her legs were not strong enough to bear her weight; she was unable to straighten her knees; she needed to be moved with a hoist; she was able to walk to the lavatory with support; she was unable to walk to the lavatory; she was being uncooperative over walking. I gained the impression from one of the nurses that there was not much sympathy afforded her. During these conversations I made it clear that Prince's Manor was not a nursing home, and that I was becoming concerned that my aunt's condition was such that she either needed to undergo rehabilitation or that, on discharge, she should go to a nursing home.

On 20th December I was advised that Eileen could be discharged that afternoon, but that it would probably not be appropriate for me to collect her; she would instead be transported by ambulance. I explained, yet again, that Prince's Manor was not a nursing home and asked whether it would not be more desirable for her to undergo rehabilitation. I was told that rehabilitation was only suitable if the patient was a willing participant; this was not the case with my aunt as she was difficult. I found this strange as, except with regard to her savings, she was not a difficult person. I stressed that, if she was to be moved to Prince's Manor by ambulance, the hospital should ring me at least 30 minutes beforehand so that I could drive there and be present when she arrived. I was told that an ambulance had been booked for 2:00 pm, but there could be a delay and I should not set off for Prince's Manor until the hospital rang me. I was also told that the medications were unlikely to be available at 2:00, so I agreed to collect them from the hospital later. Shortly afterwards, Angela rang the hospital and was told that Eileen was due to leave at about 3:00. As I had heard nothing further, I rang the ward at 5:20 only to learn that she had left about ten minutes earlier. I was also told that I would still have to collect the medications. No explanation was given as to why they had not gone with the ambulance. The excuse for not telephoning me was that the ward was very busy.

Anna and I drove to the hospital to collect the medications, and from there to Prince's Manor. On arrival, the duty manager expressed her concern at my aunt's physical state, and Anna and I were horrified at Eileen's deterioration over a short period of time. She was frailer than ever, skeletally thin, immobile and had severe bruising on the inside of her right arm, which was partially covered by a bandage. The manager was so concerned at this that she rang the ward to enquire about its cause but was told that there was no reference to it in her notes.

The care home carried out an assessment the following morning and advised me that my aunt's condition was so poor that she would have to be transferred to a nursing home. I also learned that she was now doubly incontinent. They found it extraordinary that the hospital had seen fit to discharge her. I was told that my mother had briefly seen her sister and had been reduced to tears. However, by the next day, she had forgotten all about it.

On 22nd December, Eileen was moved by ambulance and stretcher to a private nursing home. I spent about two hours there in meetings with the manager and the matron to deal with the terms of Eileen's stay and the admission procedures. An assessment was carried out the next morning in conjunction with a doctor. He was concerned that Eileen may have suffered spinal cord compression, and I was informed that it would be necessary for her to be readmitted to the hospital for tests. I asked whether she could go elsewhere as I was very concerned at the treatment she had received there. I was, however, told that it would have to be the same hospital as it had her notes.

The next day my aunt was admitted to a different ward at the hospital. She had a CT scan which, although indicating that there was no spinal cord compression, revealed that there could be neurological damage and the hospital was investigating this further. She remained in hospital until mid-January.

*

Andrew, Morag and Emily stayed with us for Christmas. On Christmas Eve all five of us went to visit Mother at Prince's Manor. She could not, as usual, work out the relationships between us, but she responded well to Emily, who would be two in a fortnight.

*

That afternoon, four of us (Anna remained at home to do some cooking for the following day) visited Eileen in hospital. She was in a very poor state.

In the period between Christmas and New Year, I had several telephone conversations regarding Eileen with the hospital, her care agency, the nursing home, Pat and Angela. I also wrote a four-page letter to the hospital complaining about her disgraceful treatment. My correspondence with the hospital went on for almost six months and included matters I mention in the next chapter. There was little they said in this time that caused me to alter my views. In fairness, they did apologise for several aspects of their conduct. The hospital is an NHS foundation trust. If the standards it displayed in Eileen's case are typical, I pity the patients in hospitals which have not achieved that status.

Chapter Fifteen

2012

Anna and I visited Eileen in hospital on 2nd January. She was cheerful and felt that she was being well looked after. She kept wiggling her toes and said that she had been walking in the ward. The duty nurse later informed me that that was not the case. She said that Eileen was complaining about numbness in her legs and that she would probably be seeing a neurologist.

*

On 4th January I went to see Mother. Her hearing was particularly bad, and her eyesight appeared to have deteriorated. I spoke to two of the senior staff and requested that these be checked. This visit was one of the occasions that she thought that I lived at Prince's Manor and that she was visiting me in my room.

*

As it was unclear how long Eileen would be in hospital, the room at the nursing home was retained at a cost of over £950 per week. I was concerned at this continuing expense and was in a quandary over whether or not to terminate the contract. I had several telephone conversations with Angela, the hospital and the nursing home between the 4th and 6th of January. On 9th January I rang the hospital and spoke to a registrar. I explained my dilemma and he gave me a helpful summary of my aunt's condition. When I enquired as to a likely date for discharge, he told me that there were no immediate plans for that. In those circumstances, Angela and I took the decision to terminate the contract with the nursing home in the hope that there would be a room free when Eileen was eventually discharged. I telephoned the home that morning and, the same afternoon, Anna and I went there to remove Eileen's possessions from her room. Within an hour of arriving back at our house, I received a telephone call from a nurse at the hospital who informed me that my aunt's consultant wished to discharge her to the nursing home, apparently on the basis that the hospital could not do anything further for her. I protested very strongly, explaining the events of earlier that day and asked to speak to the consultant. He had apparently left for the day, but the nurse said she would try to contact him on his mobile. In the meantime, I rang the nursing home, but the manager had already left. I was informed that she had seen somebody else that afternoon who was interested in taking the room.

The nurse rang back to report that she had spoken to the consultant who had requested the registrar, to whom I had spoken that morning, to telephone me. I was informed that he was in a clinic but would ring me that evening. He had apparently told the nurse that he did not want my aunt to be discharged until a further neurological test had been carried out. The nurse, who was utterly charming throughout, admitted being somewhat confused. That made two of us. She assured me that my aunt would not be discharged until we had somewhere for her to go. She also told me that Eileen was about to be moved to yet another ward.

The registrar did not telephone me that evening, and I was left feeling very concerned that Eileen might not be able to return to the nursing home. Fortunately, I was able to retrieve the situation when I spoke to the manager the following morning. I also rang the registrar, who was unavailable but later called back and spoke to my wife. He agreed that I had received mixed messages, saying that this is what sometimes happens when there are doctors of different disciplines involved. He confirmed that he wanted to conduct further tests and my aunt would therefore be remaining at the hospital for several more days. I think that the registrar was being diplomatic. The consultant was aware that another doctor, working in a different specialism, was also involved in my aunt's treatment. To have failed to liaise with him over Eileen's discharge demonstrated a lack of professionalism.

On 11th January I drove to the hospital for a discussion with one of the medical team on Eileen's ward. Reference was made to Guillain-Barré Syndrome being the possible cause of the tingling in her legs.

Between 11th and 15th January, I created an expanded filing system for Eileen's papers. Even after discarding a lot, they still filled five lever-arch or large ring folders.

On 13th January, a staff nurse telephoned, and informed Anna that Eileen was medically fit for discharge. She said that the nursing home was happy to have her back and that the hospital wanted to discharge her that afternoon. It was agreed that I would ring back later. When I returned home, I telephoned the manager at the nursing home who, after making various enquiries, informed me that the hospital had not been in touch. In any event, it was the home's standard practice to carry out an assessment before admitting or re-admitting a patient. It therefore seems that the hospital, in its eagerness to be rid of Eileen, may have been economical with the truth. The assessment would be carried out the following Monday. I rang the staff nurse to inform her of this.

*

Anna and I went to see Mother on 15th January. We made no mention of Eileen's state of health.

*

The following day, I took back to the nursing home Eileen's clothes and other belongings that I had removed on 9th January.

On 17th January, Anna and I drove to Eileen's flat where we did a lot of clearing up. We collected some more of her clothes which I later took to the nursing home. Eileen was moved back there by ambulance the same day. She looked terrible.

I went to see her again two days later. The home had provided her with a television which was on, but she was dozing when I arrived. When she awoke she was unable to find her spectacles, not realising that they were on her bedside table. She seemed to perk up when she put them on and was able to see the TV properly. The assessment the home had carried out did not reveal anything new. As at the hospital, she had a catheter. Unfortunately, she had yet another urinary infection, probably exacerbated by her failure to drink enough. She was still eating very little. The senior nurse informed me that Eileen would be seeing a physiotherapist the following morning and, subject to the latter's advice, the home would try to get her into a wheelchair with a view to her going into the lounge and dining room.

As it was now apparent that Eileen was unlikely to be returning to her flat, I completed a form for exemption from Council Tax and partially completed an application form for the higher rate of Attendance Allowance. She was already in receipt of the lower rate. I needed additional information from the nursing home to enable me to complete this, and so I went there for a meeting on the afternoon of 24th January with a staff nurse. Eileen was dozing and seemed unable to wake up properly. The nurse had already sent for the doctor. I remained at the home so that I could speak to him. After examining Eileen, he advised me that she was close to death. I returned home and rang Angela. Shortly afterwards the nurse telephoned me to say that Eileen had died.

In her last few weeks Eileen had been shunted from pillar to post; she was very confused as to her whereabouts and what was happening to her. I gained the strong impression that, during her last two periods at the hospital, her various moves were merely to suit its convenience. This also resulted in her being under the care of a variety of consultants so that nobody appeared to be in control of the situation. On the other hand, I have nothing but praise for the nursing home.

Later that afternoon and the next day I was busy with various jobs, such as notifying members of the family and the warden of the sheltered accommodation of Eileen's death; contacting funeral directors; collecting Eileen's belongings from the nursing home; collecting the death certificate; meeting with the funeral directors; and registering the death at the registry and with Eileen's bank. In subsequent days I had to notify people of the funeral details and arrange a reception afterwards.

My mother was never told that her sister had died. There was no point in doing so.

Early on the Saturday morning following the death I drove, with Anna, to Eileen's flat to continue clearing out her stuff. A problem had arisen in that Eileen had specifically requested that her ashes should be scattered with Bob's. Nobody knew, however, where she had kept those. I eventually found them in a box at the back of her wardrobe among several shoe boxes. I also came across several more documents that Eileen had squirrelled away. My clearing tasks were far preferable to the job which my poor wife had volunteered to do, which was to clean the bathroom. In the bath was a bucket in which soiled underwear had been left to soak by the carers. It had been there for weeks and, when Anna emptied it, the stench permeated the flat. It was a revolting job that made her feel physically sick.

*

The funeral was arranged for 2nd February. The day before, I collected my aunt and uncle, June and John, and their daughter, Alison, from the station. They were staying with us for a couple of nights. In the afternoon I took them to see Mother. She did not understand who any of us were. She thought I was her brother and had no idea as to the identity of the other three. At one stage, when June explained that she was her sister, Mother replied: "I have a sister June, but you are not her." She could probably only remember June as a much younger person.

*

Eileen had a wanted a religious service at her cremation and had left notes of her choice of the reading and music. The funeral directors recommended a retired clergyman to conduct the service. Angela emailed me some brief information on Eileen's early life which I forwarded to the ex-vicar. I also spoke to him on the phone to provide some details of more recent events and to give him an idea of Eileen as a person. I explained that some of this was simply for his information and was not to be used in his funeral address. Unfortunately, I had not appreciated that he was well past his use-by date. His address at the service was an embarrassment. Not only did he get things wrong, but he also included matters I had told him not to. To make matters worse he thanked Angela for providing the background information. I sat there wishing I was somewhere else.

On the afternoon of 3rd February, I had an appointment at my local branch of Eileen's bank with the person I had seen when registering the death. I was informed, however, that he had moved to another branch. The woman I saw in his place could not find the documents he had copied at our meeting. Fortunately, I had brought the originals with me again and she copied those. She apologised for the inconvenience.

I handed over a form that Angela and I had signed at the bank's request. The woman then informed me that her colleague should have given me a second form by which we applied for an executors' account. I complained that, if I had been provided with that form, I could have got Angela to sign it at the funeral yesterday. This was met with a second apology. The myriad of ways in which my aunt's bank had demonstrated its incompetence throughout my dealings with it was remarkable.

Anna and I returned to Eileen's flat on 16th February to continue cleaning the place and clearing out stuff. I also had a meeting with a local firm of estate agents with a view to marketing the property.

*

The following day I visited Mother. On this occasion she knew that I was a member of her family but did not know how I was related to her. She did not remember my father and did not know who she herself was.

*

I instructed the solicitors, who had previously acted for Eileen, to act for the executors in their sale of the flat. On 22nd February I went to see them and handed over all relevant documents. From there I went to the flat and resumed clearing out Eileen's belongings, returning the following day with Anna to continue the process and to clean. It took much longer than I had anticipated. Neither of us thought that the place had been cleaned properly since Eileen moved in seven years earlier. All the carpets were filthy. Where we moved various items of furniture to vacuum, the colour of the carpet under where they had been was a completely different colour to the rest of it. There was a painting behind the sofa that had presumably been put there out of the way when Eileen moved in and had not been touched since. It was so thick in dust that we could not see the picture. I had to take it, and several other things, outside and use a brush on them. It was squalid, and it would have been a waste of money having the carpets cleaned; anyone moving in would almost certainly want to re-carpet throughout. It was no wonder Eileen felt ill so often as it could not have been healthy living in such conditions. Even if she did not feel up to cleaning, she could have paid a cleaner to come in for a couple of hours each week. The cleaning the care agency carried out was only superficial. Eileen had never bothered to put lampshades on the lights, leaving bare bulbs to hang down from the ceilings, despite offers from Anna and me, and also Angela and Roy, to buy some for her. She always said that she would deal with it, but she never did.

Apart from her flat and her investments, Eileen did not own anything of value. A few small items from the flat were passed to members of the family as mementos, but everything else was disposed of. It is sad that, in the course of a long life, she had acquired very little of interest to anyone else.

We are almost at the end of Eileen's story, but there are three matters arising from the administration of her estate that are worth mentioning.

Angela and I had been appointed as executors under Eileen's will. At my suggestion we were appointed on a joint and several basis. This meant that I could deal with the administration of the estate largely on my own, although I made sure that Anna was kept informed of all developments. This was done to expedite the process, although it took two years to finally wind it up. There was much more work involved than I foresaw, but the principal delay was caused by the difficulty in selling the flat. It took a year to find a purchaser and, even then, the sale nearly fell through. The purchaser was partly disabled and one of the attractions of the property for him was the existence of a stairlift serving the two flats on the first floor. When his solicitors asked our solicitors for confirmation that the landlord's consent to the installation of the stairlift had been obtained, it was discovered that it had not. The owner of the other flat, Beryl, had had the lift installed and had persuaded my aunt to share the cost, even though Eileen did not, at the time, have any need for it and, in the event, used it very rarely. It seems that it did not occur to either old lady that they needed their landlord's permission. To further complicate matters, Beryl had died about two months after Eileen and her flat had already been sold. Our solicitors requested the landlord (a housing association) to grant retrospective consent, but this was refused. Instead the landlord required the lift to be removed. I thought this was unreasonable as the existence of a stairlift would presumably have enhanced the value of the freehold. I had a considerable battle to get it to change its mind. To complicate matters further, it did not appear that Beryl's daughter, acting as executor, had transferred her interest in the stairlift to the purchaser of Beryl's flat. Eventually, I managed to resolve the dispute whereby Beryl's daughter and the purchaser of her mother's flat transferred such interest they may have had in the stairlift to the purchaser of Eileen's flat. He in turn agreed with the landlord that he would enter into a maintenance agreement with the manufacturer. Thus, the lift stayed, and the flat was sold.

The second matter arising from the administration relates to the confusion on the part of the gas supplier regarding the meters outside the building. The problem arose again in mid-2012. Things came to a head when Beryl's daughter concluded that her mother had been overpaying for years. She arranged for a meter reader to call. He carried out a test by switching on a gas appliance in Beryl's flat and seeing which meter registered the consumption. It demonstrated that Beryl had been billed for Eileen's gas and vice versa. This had worked out badly for Beryl as her gas consumption was much lower than Eileen's. Beryl's estate was refunded the excess charges and Eileen's estate was presented with a revised account for almost £800. This was, in fact, considerably less than I had been led to believe could be the case when the potential problem had first arisen, probably because a direct debit had remained in operation while Eileen was in hospital and the gas consumption was much lower. I only had the boiler operating periodically, at a relatively low temperature, in order to stop the pipes from freezing. I had several conversations with the supplier who, in recognition of the fact that the error was theirs, kindly wrote off the balance.

The third matter actually occurred after the estate had been wound up. A letter arrived from Eileen's bank reporting that, after discussions with the Financial Conduct Authority, it had been accepted that advice given regarding one of the investments in the bank's subsidiary had not been appropriate for some customers. This was the investment mentioned earlier of which I had been critical. A cheque for almost £10,250 was enclosed as compensation. That was an unexpected bonus for me and the other beneficiaries.

*

We now return to my mother who, after being comparatively pleasant for several months, had recently begun to get difficult again. Anna and I went to visit her on 1st March. We arrived in the late morning. It seemed she had only just woken up and was in a very aggressive mood. We were greeted with "Where have you come from?" She then announced that she had been beaten and robbed. When we suggested that she had been dreaming, she said "If you don't believe me, you can bugger off!" Surprisingly enough, we didn't stay long. She had not, of course, been either beaten or robbed. It was another instance of her confusing dreams for reality. Before leaving Prince's Manor, I spoke to the manager to express concern about Mother's recent behaviour.

Four days later, Prince's Manor's doctor (a GP from a local practice) telephoned me. The care home had informed him of my concerns. His view was that my mother's behaviour was due to the dementia worsening. We went on to discuss her increasing weight and problems with her vision. I learned for the first time that, in addition to cataracts, she was also suffering from macular degeneration.

Because of my mother's unpleasantness I did not visit her again until 30th March. Perhaps absence had made the heart grow fonder or, more likely, the doctor had prescribed happy pills. For whatever reason, she was remarkably cheerful. This was another occasion when she seemed to be confusing a dream with reality. She was under the impression that I worked for the Royal Family at Buckingham Palace. She was very proud of me and thought that I was bound to receive an honour soon. I didn't disillusion her.

Thereafter I resumed my fortnightly visits, Tom visiting on the weeks I did not. As usual these visits were heavy going as it was impossible to have a meaningful conversation. At least she was not hostile. Indeed, my diary records that on 26th May she was 'very happy, albeit very confused.' Anna came with me on that occasion. I think it was about this time that Mother started saying how handsome I was. This happened on several occasions. The reason for my sudden popularity was unclear. I have already mentioned the poor state of her eyesight.

On my next visit I was accompanied by Andrew, Morag and Emily. The number of times Andrew and Morag visited my mother reflects very well on them. They are both family oriented, which gives Anna and me hope for our dotage.

The state of my mother's confusion at that time is apparent from a couple of visits I made in August. On 9th August I went with Anna. During our visit, Mother veered from saying that Prince's Manor was shabby and unclean, to its being beautifully painted and very clean. Then, on 24th August, she was puzzled as to the basis on which she was at the care home. She appeared to think that she was in the process of buying the building.

On 8th September Anna and I went to the annual Prince's Manor garden party. Mother was difficult initially, refusing to leave her room. Eventually she was persuaded to do so, and her mood improved.

When I saw her on 3rd October, Mother looked terrible. She seemed exhausted and was unresponsive. I was concerned that she may have suffered another transient ischaemic attack (or mini-stroke) and so I asked Tess, the deputy manager, to have a look at her. Mother was more responsive with her. Tess said she would have her monitored for two hours; if she was no better, she would call for the doctor. We both thought it was probably a case of Mother not having had enough sleep.

Nothing worth mentioning occurred on my subsequent visits to my mother until 4th December. My diary records that she was very pleased to see me that day. That was gratifying, especially as I was informed that she had been aggressive earlier.

I next went to see Mother on Christmas Eve. Sarah came with me, although Mother, who was depressed and particularly deaf that day, probably did not know who she was.

CHAPTER SIXTEEN

2013

ANNA AND I VISITED MOTHER ON HER BIRTHDAY IN January. She had a problem with her stomach, which the home thought was caused by constipation, and was in bed. Tom arrived about ten minutes after us. Whilst we were there she fell asleep and, after a while, we left and went out to lunch.

I next went to see her the following month. Anna again came with me. She was better than me in keeping some sort of rudimentary dialogue going.

On 4th March, Tess from Prince's Manor rang me to say that my mother had had a fall while using her Zimmer frame. Her ankle had swelled up and the doctor was going to have a look at it. Mother was subsequently sent for an X-ray which revealed the ankle was fractured and it was put in a plaster cast.

Later that month I arranged for my investment managers to take over the payment of my mother's care home fees from the funds under their control. This made life easier for me as it meant that I no longer had to ensure that I had sufficient of her cash available to do so.

On 31st March (Easter Sunday) there was an extraordinary example of just how bad my mother's short-term memory had become. I went to see her with Andrew, Morag and Emily, who was, by then, three years old. We stayed about 45 minutes, during which time Emily was the main topic of conversation. Mother's questions or comments went round in a familiar loop: "What's her name?", "How old is she?", "Isn't she clever." After leaving Mother, we got as far as the front door when I realised that I had left my keys in her room. Emily came with me to collect them. As we entered her room, Mother turned to Emily and said "Hello. I've not seen you before." About a minute had elapsed since we had taken our leave.

I next went to see my mother just over a fortnight later. She was very depressed and hostile towards me. Before leaving the care home I went to discuss her condition with the manager and returned home feeling rather depressed myself. It was stressful enough having to see my mother without having to tolerate her unpleasantness and so I decided to take an extended break from these visits. I was, in any event, busy during this period with administering Eileen's estate, and sharing child-minding duties with Anna. Emily needed collecting from nursery at 5:00 pm up to four days a week and then looking after for a while until one of her parents got back from work.

My mother's care home fees were, by this time, costing just under £3,260 a month. They had increased by £304 a month since she entered Prince's Manor in January 2009. These fees were met almost entirely from her own funds. The only State contribution was the higher rate of Attendance Allowance, which I had successfully applied for in early 2009. This amounted to £70.35 a week. By 2013 it had increased to £79.15. This paid for approximately three days' fees each month.

There is an additional means of financial support for people paying nursing home or care home fees out of their own pockets. It is called NHS Continuing Healthcare. If it can be shown that a person has long-term, complex health needs, an application can be made to the NHS for Continuing Healthcare funding. If the application is successful, the NHS will pay for the fees in their entirety. Various assessments are made, and it is essential that the needs are medical as opposed to social. This type of grant is notoriously difficult to obtain.

I made an application for Continuing Healthcare in late 2012. Owing, possibly, to a breakdown in communication between the NHS and Prince's Manor, it took until 21st June for the assessment to be carried out. It was held at Prince's Manor and I attended as my mother's representative. I was expecting it to fail and those expectations were fulfilled.

I next saw Mother on 29th August with Anna and we met up with Tom there. The three of us mainly talked between ourselves. Mother was aware of a conversation going on and seemed quite content.

I visited again on 3rd October. Mother was sitting uncomprehendingly in front of the television. I tried making simple conversation but gave up after a while and watched the TV myself. Mother snoozed. When I next went to Prince's Manor, Mother was again uncommunicative, although she seemed quite content. On my visit the following month she seemed positively happy, albeit hopelessly muddled.

In December, Anna accompanied me to Prince's Manor. Mother was again in a good mood but was away with the fairies. What passed for conversation was surreal.

CHAPTER SEVENTEEN

2014

I VISITED MOTHER AT PRINCE'S MANOR ON 2ND JANUARY and met up with Tom there. Again, she seemed content to sit there while Tom and I talked to one another. As usual, he and I took the opportunity to have lunch together afterwards.

*

I have referred previously to the difficulties I experienced with financial institutions whilst acting under a power of attorney. Possibly the worst example of this occurred around this time.

On 2nd December 2013 a fixed-term bond I had taken out for my mother matured. This investment, with a High Street bank, had been made in the names of Tom and me as our mother's attorneys. At the same time as taking out the bond, the bank required us to open a savings account. The matured funds were placed in that account. I called in at the local branch on 29th November and gave instructions on what to do with the funds. Even though the power of attorney was a joint one, the bank had treated me as a sole attorney from the outset. Whilst this was clearly inappropriate, I did not raise an objection because it facilitated dealings with the bank as my brother lives over an hour's drive away. It nevertheless indicated a level of incompetence. To avoid any problems in dealing with the funds, I took the precaution of obtaining a letter of consent from Tom which I handed in to the branch.

The bank clerk explained that there would be a delay of a few days before the savings account could be closed. She also advised that the only way that the funds could be transferred to my mother's current account (with a different bank), without incurring a fee, would be by sending a cheque. In view of the amount invested, I instructed her that the funds should be transferred by CHAPS and we would bear the fee.

A week after the bond matured, the account closure team wrote to me by second class post (thus causing even more delay) saying that the account could not be closed as the request to do so was not in line with the instructions applicable to the account. They required my signature together with that of my mother. I responded by letter pointing out that if written authority from me was necessary, I should have been asked for it when I visited the branch; my mother had never been a signatory on the account; it was not until 13th December that I became aware of a difficulty in closing the savings account and, in view of the amount involved, a greater degree of urgency should have been shown, particularly as I had requested that the funds be sent by CHAPS.

At some time after Christmas I received a closing statement for the savings account. This was dated 23rd December. Thereafter I checked my mother's current account on several occasions as I was anxious to get the money reinvested.

On 6th January, I rang the branch but received a recorded message informing me that nobody was able to take the call and inviting me to ring back later. I had had the same experience on other occasions. I therefore rang the bank's support centre. After the usual lengthy wait, my call was answered, and I explained the problem. I was then put on hold whilst the matter was investigated. Several minutes later I was informed that a cheque had been posted to my mother's bank on 23rd December. I asked to which branch it had been posted and was told it was to an admin centre, but they were unable to let me know which one. I asked why the funds had not been sent electronically and was told that the bank could not do this where the amount exceeded £8,000, unless they were able to speak to the account holder. They had allegedly been unable to speak to me as they did not have my telephone number. This was, of course, abject nonsense. Firstly, the bank had had instructions in writing. Secondly, it had had my telephone number ever since the account was opened. Thirdly, the number is shown on my letter headings.

It was suggested that I should contact my mother's bank, which I then did. They had no record of the cheque having been received. I suspected that, with the level of incompetence at the paying bank, which was by then only too apparent, either the cheque was never sent, or it was sent with inadequate instructions to enable the relevant account to be identified.

I then rang the bank's retail customer service centre and spoke to an employee to whom I had to explain the problem all over again. He could not understand why the funds had not been sent by CHAPS and said he would contact the account closure team and ring me back the same day. He did not do so. The following day, 7th January, I rang him again. He indicated that he had spoken to the department in question, but they had not got back to him. He said he would contact them again. Having not heard from him, I rang him once more the following day and asked to speak to the manager of the account closure team.

He told me that there was not a manager as such, but he would ask his supervisor to speak to me. The latter did so the next morning. He apologised for what had occurred and transferred me to someone in the concerns team. She informed me that the matter would be investigated and that I should be hearing from the bank within seven days. I protested that this was yet further delay and that I wanted the problem resolved that day. If the cheque had not been presented, it should be stopped, and the funds transferred by CHAPS. I was told that the matter could not be processed more quickly for security reasons.

If the transfer of the funds had been carried out competently I should have been able to send them to my financial advisers for investment within a few days of 2nd December. As things stood, my mother had been deprived of the benefit of that investment for over a month and I had had to waste a lot of time and suffer increasing frustration.

The last telephone call did the trick. The bank called me later that day to apologise, and to let me know that they were stopping the cheque and were transferring the funds by CHAPS that day. They were also paying £100 compensation.

The incompetence of that bank almost beggars belief, but not quite. I had already had experience of Eileen's bank.

*

Later that month Mother had her 90th birthday. I usually visited her on her birthday but did not go that year as my forehead and scalp were unsightly, following some cryotherapy treatment for actinic keratoses. Tom went to Prince's Manor and reported that Mother had been placed at the head of a long table at lunch and the cook had baked her a cake. Mother was not aware of why this was happening.

I visited my mother again on 31st January, this time on my own. Fortunately, she was in a happy mood. She was also quite happy when I went on 26th February, although she was still in bed when I arrived at about 11:30. She had been unable to wash and dress herself for several years and I guess the carers had left her in bed as she was tired. If she had not been in bed, she would have either been sitting in front of the TV in her room or, if I had not been coming, dozing in an armchair or her wheelchair in the residents' lounge. Unless she was ill, she would be washed and dressed by lunchtime.

At this time, I was only visiting Mother once a month as there was almost no communication between us. I attempted conversation but usually she showed little or no inclination to talk. The April visit was different, however. She again appeared happy. As I left, she asked me to pass on her regards to my mother! It occurs to me that, on some of the occasions when she was pleasant to me, she was unsure of my identity.

Anna came with me for the June visit. My mother's hearing was particularly bad and so I spoke to the manager about it. She informed me that Mother was having olive oil drops in her ears prior to them being syringed. If that failed to help, she would be referred to an audiologist.

When I called to see my mother in July, she was not speaking at all. I was advised that she appeared to have thrush at the back of her throat, and it was probably painful to talk.

Angela and I had been in regular contact regarding Eileen's estate and she had gained the impression that Maggie was not likely to last much longer. She said that, before her elder sister died, she would like to see her again. She and Roy drove down from Herefordshire for this purpose in early August. It was largely a wasted journey as Maggie did not recognise either of them. A lot of the time she did not seem to know me either, although that appeared to change at the end of the meeting. She was not in a good mood. A young lady doctor called to see her, while we were there, to inspect her mouth or throat. Mother refused to open her mouth despite the doctor's best efforts to persuade her. Angela, Roy and I left the room for a while in the hope that our absence might assist the doctor. It did not, and she emerged, defeated, a few minutes later. I suspect that if she had been older, she might have had more success. My mother had a history of being difficult with the younger carers.

I think Angela was shocked by what happened shortly afterwards. My mother suddenly rounded on me and asked, "Why are you pulling that face?" I was unaware that I had been but, if I had, it was probably because I was straining to hear what she was saying. I attempted to explain this, but to no avail. She then turned to Angela and said, "That's the kind of person he is."

The next day I spent a lot of time working on my mother's annual claim for reimbursement of tax. I had been carrying out this task for several years in order to save her the accountant's fees. Perhaps if she had been aware of the amount of work I did on her behalf, she would have been less unpleasant.

The next time I saw Mother was in early September when Anna and I went to the Prince's Manor garden party, accompanied by Andrew, Morag and Emily. Although this took place in the afternoon, Mother was in bed when we arrived and was very sleepy. She did not appear to be physically ill. She was, as usual, fascinated by Emily but kept referring to her as if she were a boy, and twice referred to herself as a man.

A few days later I had a meeting with the manager at Prince's Manor to obtain information with a view to possibly making a second application for a Continuing Healthcare grant. Two days after that, I had a telephone call in the evening from Prince's Manor to inform me that Mother had been admitted to hospital with an obstruction to her windpipe. The hospital rang me later to say that they would keep her in overnight and investigate further the next day. By the following day the obstruction had disappeared, and she was discharged.

Later that month I had a telephone conversation with a representative of a company who assisted with applications for Continuing Healthcare grants. Although their fee was not insignificant, the benefit would be considerable if the application were to succeed. I discussed the matter with Tom, and we decided to retain the company.

I next visited my mother on 24th October. She did not seem to recognise me at first but later became affectionate. Unfortunately, the reason for this became apparent: she thought I was her husband.

The following day Mother was ill again, and Prince's Manor called in the doctor to see her. She was admitted to hospital with suspected pneumonia. It turned out to be a false alarm. It must be very difficult for doctors to diagnose ailments with patients who are unable to articulate their symptoms.

In mid-November I met, at Prince's Manor, at 1:00 pm with the representative of the company assisting me with the application for a Continuing Healthcare grant. The NHS assessor was due at 2:00 but was an hour late and, when he arrived, it became apparent that the NHS was treating the meeting as a preliminary assessment. We tried to persuade him that it should be the final assessment as an earlier, unsuccessful application had been made last year. We thought we had succeeded in doing so and the meeting went well. I did not get home until about 5:15. Unfortunately, we learned later that the NHS would still require a multi-disciplinary assessment.

On 11th December, Anna and I went to Prince's Manor to see Mother and met up there with Tom and his youngest daughter,

Ellie. Mother was very sleepy and appeared clueless as to Ellie's identity.

There was a multi-disciplinary assessment of Mother by two NHS representatives in mid-December. I attended on my own. The application for a Continuing Healthcare grant failed. Considering my mother's state of health (severe dementia, very deaf, doubly incontinent, unable to feed, wash or dress herself, and unable to get in or out of her wheelchair unaided), I asked one of the assessors how bad someone had to be in order to obtain a grant. She replied that they had to be virtually dead. This is an absurd situation. I had wasted a lot of time in making these applications and professional fees had been incurred, to say nothing of the waste of precious NHS resources. What is the point of having a grant that is almost impossible to obtain?

Chapter Eighteen
2015

Anna and I visited Mother on her birthday in January. She largely sat in silence, despite several attempts by us to make conversation with her.

Later that month I received the report (called a Decision Support Tool) from the NHS giving the reasons for their refusal to make a Continuing Healthcare grant. I sent a copy to the company that had assisted with the application. They considered it to be a shoddy piece of work and we discussed the possibility of appealing against it. I subsequently discussed this with my brother, and we decided against it on the basis that it would probably be a further waste of time and money.

I did not see Mother again until early March. She seemed happy and pleased to see me, although she did not appear to remember my name or who I was. It was a similar experience the next month when she did not recognise me and was unable to hear me at all.

In the circumstances there was little point in making these visits and I did not go again for several months. Once again, I did not think she recognised me, and her opening question was a curt "What do you want?" She was by then profoundly deaf and was unable to hear me even when I spoke directly into her ear.

The previous month one of Anna's relatives had died suddenly and unexpectedly of a cerebral haemorrhage in his mid-fifties. Life can be so bloody unfair. He had been fit, active and led an interesting life. My mother, on the other hand, was very old, ill and merely existed.

In early September I went with Anna to see my mother. She was in bed when we arrived in the late morning. She remembered my name on this occasion but did not seem to know Anna or, at least, her name. She could not hear either of us and was speaking unintelligibly. Even when we could make out what she was saying, it was nonsense.

In mid-November, Tom and I both went to Prince's Manor. I had a meeting with the managing director about various management issues, while Tom saw Mother. I only saw her for about ten minutes and was unsure whether she recognised me. In any event, she did not speak to me.

We met again at Prince's Manor a month later. This time I took Morag with me together with her younger daughter, Kirstie, who was then four months old. Mother enjoyed seeing the baby but kept referring to her as a boy. She mentioned Tom's name during our visit, but not mine.

Chapter Nineteen

2016

In early 2016 my scalp and forehead were again looking unsightly because of cryotherapy. If I needed this, I tended to have it early in the New Year when I was not particularly socially active. I was not venturing out without wearing a hat and, consequently, did not visit my mother for several weeks. Tom went to see her for her birthday (not that she was aware of it) and took her a present from the two of us.

I saw Mother twice within a few days in March. On the first occasion I went with Sarah, Jon, Millie and Maisie, who were staying with us for the weekend. Maisie had been born in April 2013. This was her first visit to her great-grandmother. Mother had been washed and dressed but then put back into bed until lunch. She said nothing and gave little or no sign of recognising any of us. She even failed to respond when Jon spoke to her in French. She probably could not hear him. Both little girls were rather scared of her.

On the second occasion, I went with Anna, Morag, Emily and Kirstie. Mother looked very frail and tired. She barely reacted to us.

Earlier that month my mother's one remaining half-sister died aged 101. They were certainly a long-lived family. I did not inform Mother of the death as I did not think it would register with her.

I went to see Mother in June, again accompanied by Anna, Morag and the two girls. Mother was lying in bed and looking very frail. She gave no sign of recognition of any of us although, belatedly, responded to Kirstie. That evening I received a telephone call from her doctor who had also been to see her that day. He thought she was fading and only had weeks to live.

When Anna and I visited Mother in August, she was asleep for the whole of the time we were with her. The next day Prince's Manor rang to say that she had died.

I notified Tom of the death and discussed what to do regarding a funeral. We knew that she wished to be cremated and that her ashes should be scattered with those of our father. We wanted to restrict the funeral to immediate family. In any event, Mother had not been in contact with any of her friends for several years. It was a long way for June and Angela to travel for the funeral and Tom and I told them that we would understand if they preferred not to come.

Tom and I met at Prince's Manor two days later to sort through and dispose of our mother's belongings. Then, over the next few days, I did what was necessary for the funeral: I had already had experience of this from when Eileen died.

The funeral took place in early September. Those present were Anna and me; Sarah; Andrew, Morag, and their two daughters; and Tom, Ruth, and their four children. It was a secular ceremony. Tom and I each gave an address, and three pieces of music, which we had chosen, were played on the crematorium's music system. I restricted my address to factual matters relating to my mother's life; I did not say what a wonderful mother and grandmother she had been, because it would have been untrue. As far as I can recall, none of those present cried, except possibly Sarah, who is a naturally emotional person. Tom had expressed the view for a while that he was unlikely to mourn Mother's death because we had lost her a long time ago. I agreed, save that I had lost her a long time before he did.

Postscript

With the benefit of hindsight and increased knowledge of the possible causes of dementia, it seems that both Maggie and Eileen were prime candidates for the illness.

In 2019 the World Health Organisation published guidelines on the Risk Reduction of Cognitive Decline and Dementia. In the Introduction, reference is made to several recent studies having shown a relationship between the development of cognitive impairment and dementia with a variety of risk factors including physical inactivity, unhealthy diets, social isolation and cognitive inactivity.

Throughout their adult lives, apart from housework, shopping, and occasional light gardening, neither Maggie nor Eileen did any aerobic exercise of consequence. Neither of them participated in any form of sport. Neither of them walked much. This was probably the case with most women of their generation. The exercise sessions Maggie went to for a short while when she was living in Hampshire merely involved gentle stretching. It was a case of too little too late.

After moving to Hampshire, Maggie was insufficiently socially engaged, her deafness making her increasingly isolated. She made no real friends. After Bob died, Eileen became almost a recluse.

I do not think that either woman was sufficiently mentally stimulated. As far as I am aware, Eileen had no particular interests or hobbies. Maggie's minor dealings in antiques came to an end when she left Sussex. Although she retained an interest in the garden of her new property, that did not extend to doing much work in it.

Finally, Eileen appeared to have little interest in cooking or, indeed, in eating. Her diet seemed neither healthy nor balanced.